DEPENDENCY THEORY REVISITED

Dependency Theory Revisited

B.N. GHOSH
Professor of Economics
School of Social Sciences
University of Science Malaysia
Penang
and
Director (Hon.)
Centre for the Study on Human Development
Leeds, United Kingdom

Routledge
Taylor & Francis Group

LONDON AND NEW YORK

First published 2001 by Ashgate Publishing

Reissued 2019 by Routledge
2 Park Square, Milton Park, Abingdon, Oxon, OXl 4 4RN
52 Vanderbilt Avenue, New York, NY 10017

Routledge is an imprint of the Taylor & Francis Group, an informa business

Publisher's Note
The publisher has gone to great lengths to ensure the quality of this reprint but points out that some imperfections in the original copies may be apparent.

Disclaimer
The publisher has made every effort to trace copyright holders and welcomes correspondence from those they have been unable to contact.

A Library of Congress record exists under LC control number:

ISBN 13: 978-1-138-73416-6 (hbk)
ISBN 13: 978-1-138-73415-9 (pbk)
ISBN 13: 978-1-315-18738-9 (ebk)

Contents

List of Figures

List of Tables

Prefatory Note

The theories examined here though basically Marxist in origin do manifest a good bit of aberration from the classical Marxist proposition that the introduction of capitalism does increase the production of output and it is a progressive mode of production. The theories considered in this volume broadly uphold the view that induction of capitalism has been *prima facie* responsible for the accentuation of underdevelopment in less developed countries (LDCs). The writers who maintain this strand of thought are often labelled as *radicals* for their views which are apparently opposed to conservative Marxist tenets. But since radicalism has its roots in Marxism in the context of the theories of development and underdevelopment, the theories presented by these scholars can be christened as Marxist, or still more appropriately, Neo-Marxist radical theories. It is possible to have a reconciliation of the notion of capitalist underdevelopment with traditional Marxist views on capitalism.

Following the Marxist approach, a group of scholars, mainly from Latin America, have tried to explain development and underdevelopment with reference to and as functions of world capitalism. The approach contends that as a result of the integration of LDCs with the world capitalist system, the surplus of these poor countries has been taken away willy nilly by the developed capitalist countries (DCs). The consequence is obvious: the LDCs have remained underdeveloped and the DCs have become developed. So, poverty and wealth have been churned out simultaneously by the same system of world capitalism. The dependent LDCs became poorer and the DCs became richer.

However, though initially started in the Marxist tradition, the theories of dependency in many ways provided radical explanations to the problem of underdevelopment. The theories in some measure deviated from the classical Marxist tradition and are called radical theories. Paul Baran was the first propounder of the theory of *Dependency*. It was then further extended and enriched by many scholars including A.G. Frank, Samir Amin, Dos Santos and others. These individual authors have shown considerable variations in their analyses of development and underdevelopment, although basically they have remained attached to the domain of dependency paradigm. It would, therefore, be more candid to consider their contributions as theories of dependency. In the present book, I will elaborate the main theories of those authors who have broadly followed the basic tenets of the *Dependency* approach.

Radicals see the problem of underdevelopment not as something different from development, but as an integral aspect of the process of development of capitalism. Over the temporal course of history, some countries have become more powerful centres of capitalist development, and they created colonies/peripheries for ensuring cheap raw materials and markets for their finished products. In a regular and planned way, the surplus was extracted from the peripheries and amassed at the centre. Thus, whereas the centre showed the syndrome of material apoplexy, the periphery revealed anemia. While this process sustained development of the capitalist countries, it at the same time perpetuated backwardness of the poor countries. The radicals argue that the problem of underdevelopment cannot be considered in vacuum; but it must be related to the phenomenon of development of capitalist countries.

Since the time the problem of underdevelopment/development was first analysed in a radical framework in 1957 by Paul A. Baran, many Neo-Marxist or radical theories have emerged in the scenario. But unfortunately, we do not have any holistic analytical exposition and appraisal of these theories all at one place. The basic purpose of the present volume is to prepare a critical appraisal of the radical theories of development and underdevelopment. My main focus of attention has been to prepare a critical analytical exposition of the dependency theories. This has been done from Chapters Three to Seven. Needless to add, I have devoted more time and space in discussing the oft-quoted thoughts in Chapter Eight where I have dwelt on a few of the recent writers on dependency. Chapter Nine is purported to be an analysis of the contemporary issues in the dependency debate. This chapter is very crucial to prove the relevance of the dependency theory in the modern perspective.

The main objective of the present study is to critically analyse the mainstream dependency theories and to present an overview of the contemporary thoughts on these theories. Some pressing current issues having bearing on the political economy of dependency have also been incorporated in the book to give fresh flavour to the old dependency debate. I strongly believe that in the context of the present world development with respect to technology transfer, brain drain, capital movements across the world and globalisation, dependency theory can be of much use as an analytical method or model to explain the increasing inequality between the DCs and LDCs. The dependency paradigm is still relevant as a partial explanation of development and underdevelopment, although it might not be the only explanatory full-blown theory.

In the seventies of the last century, some scholars pronounced the demise of the theory of dependency. However, it was a sheer mistake of fact. A theory, in a sense, is never completely discarded in social sciences. The main message of the present book is that the phenomenology of dependency may not constitute a complete and perfect theory, but as a methodology of analysing development/underdevelopment, the theory of dependency will always remain important and relevant. This is borne out by the present international economic relations between the developed and developing countries.

In exposing these theories, I have concentrated mainly on three facets: *first*, to bring out the full analytical prowess and implications of each theory/paradigm; *second*, to give the basic tenets of every theory in detail followed by a pithy summary, and *lastly*, to prepare a critical appraisal of every theory. Wherever useful, I have taken the help of charts and tables.

I verily believe that any academic study having this type of ontology which attempts to present an analysis of the original author's views along with a critique, as the present book does, is beset with a number of problematics, both at conceptual plane and also at analytical plane. It becomes really rather difficult to maintain an Olympian detachment throughout in highly controversial academic pursuits. However, as far as possible, I have tried to maintain a neither-praise-nor-bury academic position to make appraisal of these theories.

Last but not the least, I must mention a couple of limitations of the present book, which are perhaps true for any book of this genre. *Firstly*, it has not been possible for me to include the contributions of all the authors who have illuminated on development and underdevelopment from the Neo Marxist or Radical perspectives. However, I am sure I have been able to accommodate within my analytic umbrella most of the more important and celebrated authors. *Secondly*, non-availability of materials has remained a colossal stumbling block. This perhaps is the reflection of both the cause as well as the effect of the phenomenon of underdevelopment *per se*. Stock of published knowledge (information) is not only meagre in LDCs but its flow is also constrained in a number of ways. Sub-optimality in every direction is the obvious outcome. I am pained to confess that in spite of my best possible efforts, I could not catch hold of all the writings of every author I have chosen to discuss in the book. Some of the highly esoteric writings of some theorists published in highly localised house journals could not be made available. My language constraint has also not enabled me to go through the original articles in languages other than English. I had to remain content with the translated works.

Be that as it may, I presume that I have been able to present the meat of the matter of every theory in a rather simple fashion without any Humpty-Dumptyness. In the preparation of this book, I have drawn materials rather liberally from many books and journals. Their names are mentioned at the end of every chapter and also in the *Bibliography* at the end of the book. I owe a debt of gratitude to all of them for the help that they have rendered. I also feel indebted to my friends both in Malaysia and India for various types of external effects which have produced many positive pay-offs for this project. Their names are too numerous to be mentioned in the *Introduction*. My colleagues in the Department of Economics, Universiti Sains Malaysia (Penang), in particular, Dr. Lai Yew Wah, Haji. Ismail Omar, Dr. Abdul Fatah Che Hamat, and Dr. Suresh Narayanan have helped in wriggling me out of many a fuzzy problem that confronted me from time to time while writing this book. My gratitude is also due to Professor Syed Ahmad Hussein, Dean, School of Social Sciences, Universiti Sains Malaysia, for his positive encouragement and also for providing me with a very congenial milieu for completing the present study. I am thankful to Marina Cheah and Abdul Hamid for their assistance in the preparation of this volume. The book owes its origin to my post-graduate students of *Political Economy* at the Department of Economics, Panjab University, India, with whom I had discussed most of the topics of this book while giving them the course on *Political Economy*. I am thankful to all these budding political economists for their encouragements and suggestions. However, none is responsible for the remaining mistakes and lapses, if any, and the usual caveat applies here as well.

B. N. Ghosh
University of Science Malaysia
11800 Penang, MALAYSIA
Email: <ghosh@usm.my>

1 The Ontology of Dependency

What is Dependency?

Dependency is a form of unequal international relationship between two sets of countries. One set of countries is called the centre or metropolitan centre, and other set of countries is called the periphery or satellite. The centre represents developed capitalism and the periphery represents underdeveloped region. Dependency is a type of mechanism which can explain the causes of economic development and underdevelopment. The theory of dependency considers the fact that the social and the economic development of less developed countries (LDCs) is conditioned by the external forces which are nothing but the central capitalism. The metropolitan countries are more powerful capitalist countries but LDCs are weaker and they also do not have the full-boiled capitalism. According to the dependency theory, underdevelopment can be explained by the fact of relations of dominance over the LDCs.

The Historicity

The theory of dependence, in a sense, is originally Marxian in character, because it is based on the concept of exploitation of the weaker LDCs by the capitalist DCs. *Secondly*, it is Marxian in the sense that it explains development and underdevelopment with reference to capitalistic framework of the centre. The theory was first popularised by Paul Baran in 1957 in his book, *The Political Economy of Growth*. Baran is regarded as the father of modern dependency theory. After Baran, it was subsequently developed by many other illustrious scholars like Frank, Samir Amin, Emmanuel, Furtado and others. It must be pointed out that although the theory of dependency originally started as a Marxist theory, later on many changes were incorporated into the theory, which departed significantly from the classical Marxist proposition. For example, the theory of dependency, unlike the classical Marxist theory, is analysed in terms of exchange relations and not in terms of production relations. Thus, in a

1

sense, a dependency theory cannot be called a proper Marxist theory. However, it is regarded as Neo-Marxist or a Radical theory. There are many writers who have contributed to the development of the theory of dependency. But, there are considerable variations in their attitude and explanation of the basic postulates of the theory, and they also significantly differ from one another in terms of many nuances of the theory. However, one can still find some general trend and thematic similarity of many writers on certain broad and basic positions. In the present analysis, we will stick to this broad thematic presentation.

The theories of dependency, as given by scholars, are mainly concerned with the impact of imperialism and neocolonialism on the economies and society of LDCs. The theory of dependency, it is claimed, can explain the global operation of the capitalist system during the neocolonial era, while accounting for the presence of some colonial features of LDCs, and the dependence of LDCs on the DCs for the development of their poor countries.[1] Dependency arises because "....some countries can expand through self-impulsion while others, being in a dependent position, can only expand as a reflection of the dominant countries, which may have positive or negative effects on their immediate development...".[2] According to Dos Santos, dependency is a conditioning situation in which the economies of one group of countries are conditioned by the development and expansion of other more powerful and developed group of countries.[3] Dependency theorists inquire into the reasons for such economic dependency when these countries have political independence.

In Marxist tradition, the genesis of dependency theory can be sought in the failure of the theories of imperialism to explain the underdevelopment of LDCs. Bodenheimer, in this context, defines dependency as the obverse side of a theory of imperialism.[4] As pointed out earlier, dependency theory is rooted in Marxist tradition where dependency has been distinguished as a formal theory of underdevelopment in contradistinction to a concrete situation of dependency.

Macrocosmic and Microcosmic Systems

In the theory of dependency, we have the juxtaposition of two systems: macrocosmic system and microcosmic system. The macrocosmic system represents world capitalism which is controlling and influencing its sub-system or microcosmic system.

Distinctions Between Microcosmic System and Macrocosmic System

Microcosmic system	Macrocosmic system
Pre-capitalist in orientation	Capitalist in orientation
Poor and backward	Advanced and rich
Producer and exporter of primary products and importer of finished products and technology	Producer and exporter of finished manufactured products and technology, and importer of raw materials and primary commodities
Capital-poor system, its surplus is extracted by the macrocosmic system	Capital-rich system. Its surplus comes from the microcosmic system
Labour is abundant and cheap	Labour is scarce and costly
Since wage is very low at home, and high in DCs, unit import cost is high and export cost is low (unequal exchange working against the system)	Since domestic wage is high, and wage in micro system is low, unit import cost is low and unit export price is high (unequal exchange working in favour of the system)
Cannot develop itself for want of technology and capital	Already developed, and supplies capital and technology at high prices to the micro system
Exploited by the macrocosmic system	It is not exploited by any system
It is dependent on the macrocosmic system	It is more or less independent

The macrocosmic system is economically more powerful, stronger and better organised. It is important to analyse the dependency from the point of view of internal structure (microcosmic system) and external structure (macrocosmic system). However, there are contradictory relations between the microcosmic system and the macrocosmic system. Gradually the macrocosmic system influences the microcosmic system. Dependency theory speaks of dichotomy or a double system – one subsumed under the other, where the relation between the two is necessarily antagonistic – a two-system zero-sum game i.e. the gain of the macro system is the equivalent loss of the micro system. By implication, in such a situation, the study of underdevelopment of the weaker micro system is very much related to the stronger system. But the micro system cannot exploit the macrocosmic system because it is already subsumed under the larger

3

macrocosmic system. The idea is that the micro system cannot derive any gain from the macro system. We can now point out some important distinctions between the peripheral microcosmic system and central macrocosmic system, as in the following chart.

In such a schematic world structure, the surplus is extracted from the subsumed and dependent microcosmic system by the macrocosmic system. Thus, there is apoplexy in the centre and anemia at the periphery. This explains, at least partly, as to why the periphery is underdeveloped. There is no other way for the periphery but to be dependent on the centre. It cannot voluntarily snap its ties from the centre. However, dependency, unless it is forced, implies that the dependent country is getting at least some indirect benefits, though temporary from the centre, although the benefits may be more than swamped out by exploitation. Ultimately, the LDCs are impoverished due to the backwash effect generated by the actions of the centre. But there is no spread effect which can help the peripheral countries.

These two effects require a little elaboration. When two regions (namely, the centre and the periphery), are developing side by side, the stronger and the more powerful region (i.e. the centre) will draw away resources, both physical and human from the weaker and the less powerful region (i.e. the periphery). As a result, a growth-retarding backwash effect would be produced in the region where from the resources are drawn away. Backwash effects imply unfavourable effects. The backwash effects are generally produced through three factors: migration, capital outflow and unequal trade. These factors become favourable for the centre, but unfavourable for the poor peripheries.

A developing region (centre) will produce some adverse effects (backwash effects) which will be reflected on the neighbouring poor region (periphery). Backwash effects, a la Gunnar Myrdal, refer to total cumulative effects that are caused by the process of circular causation between the economic and non-economic factors. The growth of the centre, however, should produce some good effects for the peripheries with respect to technology, demand, market, knowledge and so on. These favourable effects may be called the spread effects of development. These effects can produce new growth momentum for the poor peripheries. But this is possible only when the growth-retarding backwash effects are outweighed by the positive spread effects. This is not really happening for the peripheral poor countries.

4

When a peripheral country is integrated with the world capitalist system, the world is polarised into two: centre and periphery. The centre draws away the surplus from the periphery, and as a result, the centre becomes developed and the periphery becomes underdeveloped. Thus, development and underdevelopment are the two processes of the same world-wide integrated capitalist system. Underdevelopment can be explained as a historical stage of capitalist development. Development of the periphery is possible only when its relationship with the centre is snapped. Underdevelopment can be explained in terms of the relations of domination in exchange. The domination is manifested mainly in extracting the surplus from LDCs. The result of such a dependency is the widening inequality between DCs and LDCs.

The Nature of Dependency and Exploitation

But how does a periphery become dependent on the centre? The dependency of the periphery is manifested in various ways. *First*, LDCs are dependent on DCs for technology. *Second*, the LDCs are dependent on DCs for economic and financial aid. *Third*, the balance of payments problems require the help from the DCs. *Fourth*, the LDCs cannot follow an independent policy of capital accumulation. *Fifth*, LDCs are dependent on DCs for selling raw materials and their primary products. *Lastly*, without the help of DCs, it is almost impossible for the LDCs to develop economically. Indeed, one can make a detailed menu of various types of dependency relations which have not yet been subjected to comprehensive analysis. In what follows, I provide a rather conservative list of some of the neglected areas of dependency relations which necessitate careful and detailed research for better comprehension and appreciation:

(i)   *Academic Dependency:* The education system of LDCs, including curricula, evaluation process and the like, are dependent on the Western education system. In LDCs, the stock and flow of our knowledge, thinking process, academic information and orientation, and also the dimensions of our problems and the suggestions for their possible solutions are based on western books and journals published by a few multinational publishing companies.

(ii)   *Cultural Dependency:* The socio-cultural way of life and the value system of LDCs have become completely dependent on those of DCs. The cultural dualism produced this way has led to a crisis of identity in LDCs.

(iii)   *Financial Dependency:* This refers to the dependency of LDCs with respect to capital inflows, direct foreign investment, loans, interest on loans, and so on.

(iv)   *Market Dependency:* The LDCs are dependent on DCs for various market interactions. To some extent, the domestic inflation rates and currency values of LDCs also depend on DCs. In international transactions, the LDCs have to submit to the market power of DCs.

(v)   *Human Resources Dependency:* The training of high quality manpower and the ultimate loss of a part of this manpower, commonly known as Brain Drain problem, is the reflection of a dependency relation through which human capital resources are drawn away from LDCs without the payment of compensation.

(vi)   *Consumer's Dependency:* The tastes, preferences and the consumption patterns of Third World consumers are nowadays very much dependent on DCs, their way of life and systems.

(vii)   *Bio-dependency:* The whole field of medical research, human pathology, medicines and treatment processes in LDCs are almost completely dependent on the Western system which dumps not only costly medicines but also banned and harmful drugs to the LDCs.

(viii) *Environmental Dependency:* The DCs are emerging as the vector of environmental protection. For the evaluation and solution of their pollution problems, the LDCs are made to be dependent on DCs.

(ix)   *Military Dependency:* These days, the LDCs have to remain dependent for their so-called securities on the DCs who supply the arms and ammunitions for fighting wars and frighten away the enemies if needed. But more often than not, the DCs try to sustain the bones of contention among the LDCs to make them dependent in many ways to DCs.

(x)   *Policy Dependency:* The DCs are directly or indirectly interfering with the internal policies of LDCs in the pretext of performance evaluation required to qualify as borrowers from international institutions, or for aid and assistance. The internal economic, social and political processes and policies of LDCs are influenced by and dependent on DCs.

However, although the LDCs are apparently getting some help from the centre, it is not without cost. Sometimes the cost is extremely high. In other words, DCs have been exploiting the LDCs in many ways: *First*, the DCs are investing capital in LDCs where the marginal productivity of capital is very high, and are drawing out a large amount of surplus. *Second*, the DCs are able to purchase raw materials and primary products from LDCs at low rates mainly because of the fact that wage level is very low in LDCs. Thus, through unequal exchange, the DCs are getting surplus labour values from LDCs. *Third*, DCs are able to sell out their products in LDCs at high prices. *Fourth*, the DCs are getting as remittances from LDCs large sum of money in the forms of profit, royalty and so on. *Fifth*, the technology which is being transferred to LDCs is mostly old and obsolete, unsuitable and very costly. *Lastly*, the DCs are also exploiting the LDCs through the imposition of control over the domestic economies of these poor countries through aid and other means. The DCs are also influencing the poor countries' internal economic policies. Thus, in many ways, the DCs are exploiting the LDCs. The basic way in which a periphery is exploited is through the mechanism of surplus extraction. Surplus is extracted in mainly two ways. One way is the non-trading way or direct way of extraction of surplus. This is done by looting and plundering of resources from the LDCs. It also includes the repatriation of profit from these countries. The indirect way consists of unequal exchange through which surplus is extracted from the LDCs.[5] The mechanism of surplus extraction is shown in the following chart.

Mechanism of Surplus Appropriation

	Direct Method	*Indirect Method*
Plundering of resources or looting	Profit repatriation and Royalty repatriation	Unequal exchange

Unequal exchange constitutes an indirect mechanism of surplus extraction. It is also called the trading method of surplus extraction. The mechanism of surplus extraction is not specific. It may be direct or indirect, as has been shown earlier. The wage level in LDCs is lower than that in DCs. This means that products can be produced in LDCs at lower cost. Accumulation in LDCs is not possible *per se*. Surplus value is produced in LDCs but it is appropriated by the centre. Due to lower wage level and under consumption, a mechanism is provided for the transfer of surplus from LDCs to DCs. Unequal exchange between these two types of countries means that more labour time is appropriate by DCs, as a consequence of profit rate equalisation.

Be that as it may, it is impossible to appreciate the dependency approach without understanding that it is essentially and mainly a reaction to the conventional North American development theories.[6] The Latin American social scientists and development theorists began to find out alternative explanations for the problems that capitalist countries were facing in the periphery of the world system in the fifties of the last century. In the course of their discussion, they focused on certain aspects of the reality which were not considered by the earlier development theorists. These aspects were related to the problem of exploitation of the periphery by the centre and the extraction of surplus from the backward periphery. In developing this type of idea, these writers obviously turned towards Marxist analysis for understanding the conflict, exploitation and the reasons for the persistence of poverty. However, in subsequent analysis, this new theory of dependency departed considerably from the traditional Marxian interpretation. This is evident from the fact that unlike Marxist analysis, the dependency theory is not based on the concept of exploitation of labour, but rather, it is based on the concept of exploitation of LDCs by the developed capitalist countries.

The Convergence in the Dependency Models

The dependency approach matured in the sixties and certain common themes began to emerge in the analysis in spite of many individual differences and polemics. In what follows, I shall now delineate the common characteristics or themes of the classical dependency theory. These are:

First, central capitalism is imposed on the periphery.
Second, surplus is extracted from the periphery. DCs exploit the LDCs.

Third, surplus extraction leads to development of the centre and underdevelopment at the periphery. It is believed that underdevelopment is not a national or endogenous problem. It is an exogenous problem. Development of periphery is conditioned by the world capitalist structure.

Fourth, there is unequal and uneven development between DCs and LDCs.

Fifth, integration with world capitalism aggravates the problem of national/international inequalities and underdevelopment.

Sixth, the trade relations between DCs and LDCs are unequal relations favouring the DCs and discriminating against the LDCs.

Seventh, LDCS have subordinate status to the DCs.

Lastly, development of LDCs is not possible unless and until the tie with the central capitalism is snapped. Socialism is regarded as the best alternative for having rapid economic development with social justice and equity.

The Epistemic Basis of Dependency Theory

The epistemological foundation of the theory of dependency is based on the perceived inter-relations between the core (centre) and the periphery. Such inter-relations are well around us to witness and are adequately brought out by the writings of Presbisch-Singer, Paul Baran and others in the mid-twentieth century. These works are based on empirical facts of many less developed countries as an explanation of their state of underdevelopment.

The theoretical edifice of the relation between the colonies and imperial power is however, based on the writings of Marx and Lenin. Marx's writings on the capitalist exploitation, expanded reproduction schema, revised views on Asiatic mode of production and so on do sufficiently indicate that there are possibilities of unbalanced and disproportionate pattern of growth between different sectors of an economy where the organic compositions of capital are not equal, and that generally speaking, the extraction of surplus value goes on increasing with the development of industrial capitalism. The creation of surplus value is a regular feature of capitalism. Capitalism survives through the extraction of surplus values. An application of this knowledge in the cases of interactions between developed capitalist countries (DCs) and the poor less developed countries (LDCs) using labour-intensive methods of production will at once give an idea how DCs can exploit LDCs by extracting their surplus.

Lenin's theory of imperialism analyses the stages of growth of capitalist form of development with uneven progress overtime. The expansion of capitalism is motivated by three important considerations: export of surplus capital, expansion of market and procurement of raw materials. For all these, the capitalist relations are extended to less developed poor countries. Needless to say, the stage of *finance capital* being witnessed since the middle of the twentieth century has been one of the main causes of financial crises in LDCs. Excess capital inflow due to loan-pushing by the DCs in the absence of sophisticated and disciplined capital market in LDCs has been one of the primary causes of financial turmoil in many such countries at the end the twentieth century.

Marx-Lenin theories of unequal development, unequal sectoral capital intensity, unequal wages and so on have provided the basis for the possibility of exploitation of the weaker countries by the stronger DCs. And abundant empirical support for such a state of affairs can be found during the days of colonial rules.

In the mid-1940s, while analysing his work at the Economic Commission for Latin America (ECLA) of the United Nations, Raul Prebisch used the concepts of core and periphery. In his conceptualisation, core or centre constitutes developed capitalist countries having stronger trade unions, higher wages, monopolistic export market for manufactured goods, lower income elasticity of demand for import, higher export prices, and so on. On the other hand, the countries representing periphery are poor countries having weak trade unions, lower wages, competitive export market with slow export growth, low export prices and higher income elasticity of demand for import. There are strong linkages and essential inter-relations between these two groups of countries, and in the bargain and deals, the core countries generally win over the periphery for many obvious reasons. The phenomenology of development differentials between these two sets of countries provides the main epistemic basis of the theory of dependency.

Dependency Studies in a Developing Country

The analysis of dependency in Malaysia has gone mainly into two different directions. At one end of the spectrum, the analysis goes the whole hog into the internal dynamics of the system as it affects caste, class, ethnicity and other related variables. The other end of the spectrum considers the problems of external dependency of Malaysia. There is now available a burgeoning body of literature on both these areas of analysis which can whet the appetite of the students of Malaysian political economy. [7]

In the areas of caste, class, ethnicity politics and society of Malaysia, commendable and careful works have been done, among others, by Michael Stenson (1980), C.E.R. Abraham (1976), V. Selvaratnam (1974), B. N. Cham (1975), L. M. Hui (1980), J. K. Sundram (1977 & 1978), S.A. Baharuddin (1979), Fatima Halim (1980), Martin Brennan (1985), Md. Amin and M. Caldwell (1977), A. Sivanandan (1979), H. Yaacob Hashim (1977) and Johan Saravanamuttu (1986).

In the realm of the analysis of external dependency of Malaysia, painstaking and serious works have been done, among others by, Khor Kok Peng (1979), J.J. Puthucheary (1976), Lim Mah Hui (1976), Lim Chong Yah (1967), Lee Hock Lock (1974) and C.B. Edwards (1975). While others in this group of writers concentrate on some particularised aspects of dependency, such as MNCs, profits, trade diversifications, protections and the like, the work by Khor Kok Peng is based on holistic approach which considers the problem of dependency in Malaysia in its totality, and hence, deserves a thorough and patient study.

Towards an Appraisal

There are many theoretical problems with the dependency paradigm.[8] It has been pointed out that dependency analysis cannot give us a full-fledged formal theory of development and underdevelopment but it can simply provide us with guidance in the explanation of any concrete case of underdevelopment.[9] Thus, it cannot be regarded as a theory but it is simply treated as a paradigm or model. In the so-called dependency theory, the relation of dominance is pre-supposed, and it is believed that one pole can exploit the other. The theory has failed to specify thoroughly as to how wealth and poverty can be generated by one and the same force, namely, capitalism. *Second*, it is pointed out that extraction of surplus cannot cause development and underdevelopment at the same time because it is an assumed pre-condition.[10]

The theory does not say as to how the surplus is produced and appropriated, but instead, it concentrates on how it is exchanged. *Third*, the theory gives too much emphasis on the problem of exchange rather than on the problem of production. In fact, underdevelopment cannot be satisfactorily explained through exchange relations. Development/under-

11

development is essentially a production-centric problem. *Fourth*, production and appropriation of surplus is an aspect of the relationship between classes; but class analysis has been ignored. The conflict between centre and periphery, it should be noted, is in geographical terms in this theory rather than in terms of social classes. *Fifth*, the unequal exchange as a mechanism of surplus extraction has not been explained very satisfactorily either theoretically or empirically.[11] The explanation is far less convincing as an explanation of underdevelopment. The explanation that profit rate is equal in the international market in spite of barriers, protection and unequal development, is wrong mainly because of factor immobility. Even if theoretically it is assumed that factors of production are mobile internationally, a high cost does prevent such mobility among the world countries. *Sixth*, LDCs cannot grow, according to this theory, so long as they are in the grip of DCs. This has been found to be historically false. In fact, many LDCs have been rapidly developing in modern times in spite of their links with the DCs. It is ignoring the good impact of capitalism on LDCs. Bill Warren, F.H. Cardoso and others observe that capitalism does help the growth process of underdeveloped countries. The theory has over-emphasised the role of surplus extraction. The dependency relation can very well be there between two developed countries, but there may not be any perceptible act of exploitation. It is not necessary that the linkage with DCs will necessarily lead to exploitation of LDCs.

Some of the features of dependency can also be found in non-dependent economies.[12] Moreover, even the developed countries are facing the problems which are generally the characteristics of LDCs. Some of the DCs are plagued with problems like unemployment, inflation/recession and low growth. Dependency *per se* is neither a necessary nor a sufficient condition for underdevelopment. Dependency theory suffers from circularity of reasoning: a country is poor because it is dependent, and it is dependent because it is poor.[13] The theory has not provided any viable solution to overcome dependency. Bill Warren observes that its inability stems from its subjective-moralistic overtones and interest.[14] *Seventh*, Keith Griffin and John Gurley have accused the theory of neglecting the market forces.[15] They say that the theory does not present any explanation of bioformity i.e., formation of centre and periphery in terms of any market forces. The explanation is not in terms of pure economic theory. *Eighth*, according to dependency theories, capital is invested in LDCs by the DCs because rate of profit is higher there than in DCs. The resultant profit is again invested in LDCs by the same token of argument. This means that profit is not really repatriated and invested in DCs. There seems to be a lack of internal consistency in the theory of dependency.[16]

Ninth, the paradigm can also be subjected to criticism from the point of view of the neoclassical economics. The neoclassical arguments envisage that LDCs utilise the opportunities to freely choose that course of action through which they can materialise their objective functions, or maximise their utility functions. The LDCs are never forced into the deal of dependency. It is their free volition under free market conditions. And since they have chosen the condition of dependency, it implies that dependency is the best alternative for these countries which can yield maximum net benefits under the given circumstances. Dependency cannot be bad for the LDCs. Had it been so, the LDCs would not have accepted it. Evidently, for these countries, there is no better alternative. In other words, the so-called dependency must be mutually beneficial to both LDCs and DCs.

Tenth, any concept of dependency which claims to be a theory of underdevelopment must, according to S. Lall, pass a double test of showing (a) some exclusive characteristics of dependent economies, and (b) that these characteristics adversely affect the development process of these economies. But on both these counts, the theory seems to have failed.[17] *Finally*, the theory ignores the mutually overlapping caste-class structure and cultural structure which play a major role in the generation and perpetuation of poverty and inequality in LDCs. The paradigm shows essentially a North-Western perspective of mass poverty in the Third World. The dependency model is constrained by the deterministic overtones and too simplistic generalisations.

However, all the above points of criticism cannot be hurled across the board. There are many exceptions indeed. As against all castigations, it must be conceded, as Gabriel Palma realised, that dependency theory still has its utility as a methodology for analysing the micro perspective of underdevelopment in some concrete cases.[18] The theory of dependency has not only provided an alternative method of studying underdevelopment of many LDCs, it has also given new insights, raised new issues and provided new perspective for analysing the development process of the backward countries.[19]

Notes

1. Keith, Griffin and John Gurley, "Radical Analyses of Imperialism, The Third World, and the Transition to Socialism: A Survey Article", *Journal of Economic Literature*, Sept. 1985, p. 1109.
2. Dos Santo, "The Structure of Dependence", *American Economic Review*, May, 1970, pp. 289 – 90. Santos asserts that external structure (i.e. central capitalist structure) adversely affects the internal structure, and underdevelopment is the inevitable result.
3. Loc. Cit.
4. S. Bodenheimer, as quoted in Ivan Roxborough, *Theories of Underdevelopment*, Macmillan, London, 1979, p. 43. Bodenheimer's explanation of the dependency theory is based on Marxian explanation of imperialism.
5. Tom Bottomore, *Dictionary of Marxist Thought*, Oxford University Press, London, 1983, p. 115.
6. R. H. Fagen, "Theories of Development", *Monthly Review*, Sept., 1983, p. 14.
7. Michael Stenson, *Class, Race and Colonialism in West Malaysia*, University of Queensland Press, Queensland, 1980; C. E. R. Abraham, *Race Relations in West Malaysia*, Unpublished D. Phil. Thesis, University of Oxford, 1976; V. Selvertnam, "Discoloniation, the Ruling Elite and Ethnic Relations in Peninsular Malaysia", Institute of Development Studies, Discussion Paper No. 44, University of Sussex, 1974; B. N. Cham, "Class and Communal Conflict in Malaysia", *Journal of Contemporary Asia*, Vol. 5, No. 4, 1973; Lim Mah Hui, "Ethnic and Class Relations In Malaysia", Journal of Contemporary Asia, Vol. 10, 1980; Jomo Kwame Sundram, *Class Formation in Malaysia*, Unpublished Ph. D. Thesis, Harvard University, 1977; Lim Mah Hui; "Political Economy of the State in Malaysia", Paper presented at the Annual Meeting of the Association of Asian Studies, Washington, D.C., March 1980; Shamsul Amri Baharuddin, "The Development of the Underdevelopment of the Malaysian Peasantry", *Journal of Contemporary Asia*, Vol. 9, No. 4, 1979; Fatimah Halim, "Differentiation of the Peasantry: A Study of the Rural Communities in West Malaysia", *Journal of Contemporary Asia*, Vol. 10, No. 4, 1980; Martin Brennan, "Class, Politics and Race in Modern Malaysia", in R. Higgott and R. Robinson (ed.), *South East Asia*, Routledge and Kegan Paul, London, 1985; Mohamad Amin and Malcolm Caldwell, *Malaya: The Making of a Neo-Colony*, Spokesman, Nottingham, 1977; J. K. Sundram, "Restructuring Society: The New Economic Policy Revisited", Persatuan Ekonomi Malaysia Conference, 1978; M. Stenson, *Industrial Conflict in Malaysia*, Oxford University Press, London, 1980; A Sivanandan, "Imperialism and Disorganic Development in a Silicon Age", *Race and Class*, Autumn, 1979; H. Yaacob Hashim, "Development and Restructuring of Society: Some Social and Cultural Dilemmas in a Transitional Society", Published by Persatuan Ekonomi Malaysia, Kuala Lumpur, 1977; Johan Saravanamuttu, "Imperialism, Dependent Development and ASEAN Regionalism", *Journal of Contemporary Asia*, Vol. 6, 1986, Khor Kok Peng, *The Malaysia Economy: Structures and Dependence*, Marican and Sons, Kuala Lumpur, 1983; J. J. Puthucheary, *Ownership and Control in the Malayan Economy*, Donald Moore, Singapore, 1976; Lim Mah Hui, "Multinational Corporations and Development in Malaysia" (Unpublished Paper), University of Malaya, Kuala Lumpur, 1976; Lim Chong Yah, *The Economic Development of Modern Malaya*, Oxford University Press, Kuala Lumpur 1967; Lee Hock Lock, "Public Policies and Measures Towards Economic Diversification: A Critical Study of the Experience of West

Malaysia: 1957 – 1970", Ph.D. Thesis, University of Malaya, Kuala Lumpur, 1974; C. B. Edwards, *Protection, Profits and Policy: An analysis of industrialisation in Malaysia*, Ph. D. Thesis, School of Development Studies, University of East Anglia, 1975.

8.   Tom Bottomore, Op. Cit., p. 115.
9.   G. Palma, "Dependency: A Formal Theory of Underdevelopment or a Methodology for the Analysis of Concrete Situations of Underdevelopment?, *World Development*, Vol. 6, 1978, p. 911.
10. K. Griffin and John Gurley, *Op. Cit.*, p. 1113.
11. Tom Bottomore, *Op Cit.*, p. 115.
12. S. Lall, "Is Dependence a Useful Concept in Analysing Underdevelopment?", *World Development*, Vol. 2, No. 11, 1975, p. 800.
13. Loc Cit.
14. See H. Gulalp, "Debate on Capitalism and Development", *Capital and Class*, Spring, 1986.
15. K. Griffin and J. Gurley, *Op. Cit.*, p. 1113.
16. Tom Bottomore, *Op. Cit.*, p. 115. The lack of internal consistency arises from the fact that whereas the theory postulates a mechanism of profit repatriation, the logical extension of its basic tenets does not support the postulate.
17. See, S. Lall, *Op. Cit.*, p. 800.
18. G. Palma, *Op. Cit.*, pp. 911-12.
19. B. N. Ghosh, *Political Economy of Development and Underdevelopment*, Unpublished Manuscript, 1993, p. 36.

2 Karl Marx on Development and Underdevelopment

Karl Marx had never presented any ready-to-serve full-boiled theory of development and underdevelopment. However, his ideas on development and underdevelopment, which are scattered over his various writings, can help us to weave out a definite pattern for the construction of a theoretical schema in this rather nebulous area of Marxian epistemology. This is the basic desideratum of the present chapter.

The plan for the present study is as follows: The study is divided into four main sections. Section One will delineate the conceptualisation and nature of development. Section Two is devoted to the analysis of the nature and genesis of underdevelopment. Section Three seeks to analyse the process of growth in the Marxian framework and the last section makes a critical appraisal of Marxian ideas on development and underdevelopment.

On the Nature of Development

The concept of development that Marx elaborates is not the concept of pure economic development but rather the concept of social development. In Marx's schema, economic development as it appears is subsumed under societal development. Economic development and social development are mixed up categories.

Marxian theory of growth (or, development) can be christened as the *stage theory* or *evolutionary theory of* growth.[1] Marx's theory of development, like his other theories, has had a sense of historicity. In the perspective of temporal span, Marx has conceived of five distinct stages of social development. These stages are: primitive communism (often called the Asiatic society), followed by slavery, feudalism, capitalism and then communism.[2] Each of these stages has its own mode of production which is a combination of forces of production and the relations of production. The conflict between forces of production and the relations of production leads to the emergence of a new stage of development. Conceivably, Marx's concept of development encompasses a sense of dualism. Development is both an *esoteric concept* as well as an *exoteric concept.* In the *exoteric* sense, development constitutes a qualitative transformation from one stage to another, which involves a change in the existing structure of socio-economic relations. In other words, development takes place in a dialectical fashion. In the esoteric sense, development signifies the change within the same system or stage of historical development process. In this sense, development construes some internal change – change within.

At many places, Marx has conceptualised development as being tantamount to progress. The successive higher modes of production from primitive communism to pure communism are progressive epochs.[3] To Marx, progress is something discontinuous and an abrupt leap from one type of society to another, accomplished primarily through class conflict.[4] Eric Hobsbawm in a section of Introduction to Marx's *Grundrisse* argues that Marx wanted to give a *content* to history, and the content is nothing but the idea of progress.[5] Hobsbawm observes that Marx's concept of progress is objectively definable.[6] However, another concept of progress that one can encounter in the Hegelian version of Marxism is concerned with humanist goal i.e., a journey towards the emancipation of mankind from the realm of necessity to the realm of freedom. Here, Marx becomes a bit like Kant who propounded that a true ideal can never be achieved in one life, but there should be progress towards it.

Marx's concept of development is essentially production-centric. In his conceptualisation, from a certain stage in the development of social production, there arises in man's consciousness the perception of new needs and also the consciousness that it is possible to satisfy his new needs. The feeling for the new needs generates a qualitatively new phase of development.[7] Thus, the motive force behind any social change is the satisfaction of some new needs. Development process is a continuum having many linkages or stages, each of which represents a qualitatively separate entity, which is distinctly different from others. In other words, each stage is based on a qualitatively different mode of social production. Each stage has its own law of development and arises out of a dialectical process.[8] The laws of development are historically specific and can be discovered by empirical analysis.

Marx believed that capitalist development by its very nature is uneven. This was also the belief of Trotsky.[9] The inequality in the process of development mainly springs from the unplanned nature of capitalist development. The uneven nature of capitalist development had been empirically witnessed by Marx through his study of British capitalism in its growing stage. In Marx's time, capitalist process of industrialisation was confined mainly to Britain and a few regions of Europe and North America. Marx realised that development of capitalism brings about universal dependence of nations. As a matter of fact, capitalism cannot exist in one country; it creates a world market. The world market is based on the philosophy of international division of labour in which the developed capitalist countries dominate the industrial production and the poor countries become the hewers of wood and drawers of waters. Uneven development becomes a part of the process from the very outset.

On the Nature of Underdevelopment

In the Marxian perspective, underdevelopment and development are related phenomena. Underdevelopment is a stage of development. It should be borne in mind that Marx was not primarily concerned with the problems of less developed countries (LDCs), for his basic purpose was to analyse the process of capitalist development. However, he was not altogether indifferent to the problems of LDCs and their underdevelopment. His ideas on underdevelopment and the problems of LDCs can be found in newspaper articles and his private letters. From Marx's writings, one can cull out two very basic approaches to the problem of underdevelopment. We can call these approaches: (1) Structuralist Approach, and (2) Surplus Extraction Approach. Let me pursue these approaches a bit further.

Structuralist Approach

This structuralist version of underdevelopment can be found in original form in Marx's analysis of the Asiatic Mode of Production (AMP). The ideas on AMP are scattered in his various writings.[10] The Asiatic society represented many LDCs of Marx's time. These were mainly India, China, Middle East, Java, Spain, Pre-Columbian America and Tsarist Russia. India was the main focus of Marxian analysis of AMP. The structure of these societies was mainly responsible for their underdevelopment and poverty.

These societies had certain peculiar structural features: there was the absence of private property in land. Land was owned by the state but it was cultivated communally by the village population. The state had to be paid taxes or rent. The village community existed on a symbiotic cooperation

18

among agriculture, handicrafts and caste-based division of labour. Adverse climatic conditions necessitated the construction and maintenance of irrigation canals and public works for the supply of water on which agriculture was badly dependent. This made the village community heavily dependent on the state. The state itself was underdeveloped and it exercised depotism (*oriental depotism*, a la Marx) over the village community. In general, these societies were self-sufficient at the subsistence level with technological stagnation and econo-cultural isolation. The structural rigidity was one of the esoteric causes, as Marx visualised, for the perpetuation of underdevelopment and stagnation of the Asiatic societies.

However, Marx observed that British rule in India though motivated by vested interest, was responsible for the growth of many industries and of communication facilities like railways. Western imperialism was responsible for the only social revolution ever heard in Asia.[11] Marx seems to have rationalised Western imperialism in eastern countries – the so-called *white man's burden*. In Marx's view, vicious circle of underdevelopment and stagnation in the Asiatic societies could be broken only through the destruction of AMP by capitalism. A similar view has been expressed by a Soviet historian, V. I. Pavlov. Pavlov has argued that AMP made it impossible for the inchoate capitalism from developing into modern industrial capitalism.[12] An Indian historian has also supported Pavlov's view. [13]

However, Marx in his later life challenged the salutary role of railways in British India, and also repudiated his theory of AMP or his ideas regarding the role of imperialism in promoting capitalism in the East.[14] In his later years, Marx questioned the regenerating role of British capital and trade in India and corrected his earlier stand of the double mission hypothesis – destruction and regeneration of British capital.[15] But Marx did not explain as to how capitalism could be developed in the absence of Western imperialism. Towards the end of his life, Marx admitted the possibility of the Russian commune for the direct transition to socialism without passing through the procrastean bed of capitalist process of industrialisation. But the same was not possible for the Asiatic villages as these were fundamentally different from Russian communes. Be that as it may, Marx's analysis of AMP has been the target of a number of criticisms some of which will be dealt with in the last section of the discussion.

Surplus Extraction Approach (SEA)

Like the structural approach to underdevelopment, the surplus extraction approach (SEA) was first introduced by Karl Marx in his analysis of underdevelopment. The generation of surplus value is the *differentia specifica* of capitalist system of production. But the falling rate of profit in the long-run, consequent on the increasing organic composition of capital, sets a limit to economic growth. There are many ways to counteract the falling tendency of the rate of profit. One such way is the foreign trade through which cheaper raw materials could be obtained and finished goods could be profitably disposed of. But the trade must be based on *unequal exchange*, and this would be possible if trade is carried on with colonies. Thus, expansion of colonialism becomes the ultimate safety valve for capitalist development. The existence of colonies will also ensure higher return on capital investment and the uninterrupted extraction of surplus value from the colonies.

Marx observed that as a result of colonial exploitation and deliberate policy of world capitalism, one part of the globe remains agricultural and supplier of raw materials to the other part which remains mainly industrial.[16] Needless to say, as a result of exploitation and extraction of surplus, colonies become poorer and more underdeveloped.

It is, thus, clear that Marxian theory of underdevelopment is based on his ideas on imperialism. But, unfortunately, Marx did not elaborate his ideas on imperialism. Lenin extended Marxian ideas to explain underdevelopment in terms of his theory of imperialism.[17] However, Marxist-Leninist theory of imperialism can be constructed in such a way that it can explain simultaneously development and underdevelopment as two sides of the same process and not two different stages of the development process of an economy. According to this view, underdevelopment of colonies is mainly due to the imperialist penetration of these colonies. Capitalist exploitation is the main cause of underdevelopment. Thus, SEA approach has remained the basic explanation for the underdevelopment of colonies in the Marxian analysis.

The two approaches to underdevelopment outlined above (structuralist approach and surplus extraction approach) have one thing in common and one thing uncommon. Whereas underdevelopment due to structural characteristics is essentially natural and congenital, underdevelopment due to surplus extraction is essentially man-made and capitalism-induced.

20

However, in both the cases, the induction of capitalism from abroad would perpetuate the process of underdevelopment.

It is intriguing to note that in Marx's analysis, both development and underdevelopment have esoteric and exoteric counterparts. Both are in relational construct and both are worsened by imported capitalism. The following chart is designed to highlight some of the important comparative elements of the Marxian ideas on development and underdevelopment.

Comparative Elements in Development and Underdevelopment

Development/ Under-development	Nature		Approach to Study	Relations with Under-development and Development	Role of Imported Capital-ism
	Esoteric	*Exoteric*			
Development	Development within the given system	Qualitative transformation from one stage to another	Stage theoretic (Dialectic)	Opposite supra stage of under development	Under - development of Development
Under-development	Structural Features responsible	Due to loss of surplus	(i) Asiatic Mode of Production (Structuralism) (ii) Surplus Extraction Approach	Infra Stage of Development	Development of Under - development

The Process of Growth

In the paradigm of development that Marx contemplated, forces of production become technological by their very nature, and these forces are continuously developing into higher and higher relations of production. Non-economic factors do react on the productive forces and the economic base of a society, but they originate, in the final analysis, in the techno-economic development. With the progress of man in the techno-economic field, man's consciousness also undergoes changes.

Technological progress is necessary in capitalist development for two precise reasons: *Firstly*, to augment labour productivity for producing more surplus value, and *Secondly*, to reduce cost of production so that profit rate can be increased. If profit rate declines, the wage rate must increase, as

Samuelson puts it; otherwise, technological progress would be meaningless.[18] Technological progress is ensured by capital accumulation. For the accumulation of capital, what is necessary is the sacrifice of consumption. In other words, if consumption is less out of surplus value, capital accumulation can go on increasing, and technical progress and innovation can be sustained at a higher rate. Technical progress is given so much importance by Marx in economic development that in his writings around 1880 on the development of Russia, he suggested the necessity of diffusion of technology from the Western countries.[19]

Marx's ideas on growth suggest that equilibrium growth is not possible under capitalism.[20] His analysis of reproduction schema shows that if variable capital is not invested in the required proportion, growth is disrupted by an imbalance between demand for and supply of each type of commodity. There is no correcting agency like the Planning Commission in a capitalist economy.

Marxists argue that because of the uneven development of nations, backward countries like Russia of the past, should have to adopt a pattern of forced and accelerated development combining industrial revolution with simultaneous agricultural revolution, and a struggle against feudal relations of production and archaic socio-economic formations. Different stages of historical development would have to be combined into a single telescoped stage of accelerated development.[21] This strategy has been followed by Russia and China and the contemporary backward socialist countries for breaking down vicious circles of their mass poverty.

What is implicit in Marxian connotation of development is that unless merchant capital develops into industrial capital, there cannot be any economic growth in the true sense of the term, for in that situation, the capitalist mode of production cannot be really developed. But Marx observes that two alternative paths can be taken by merchant capital: one such path may develop industrial capital and the other path may not lead to the development of industrial capital.[22]

In Marx's conceptualisation, there is dualism in LDCs in the sense that they have the simultaneous existence of capitalist sector (Department I) and subsistence sector (Department II). The former can generate surplus, and therefore, can initiate the process of growth. The key to development is that the subsistence sector must be transformed to the capitalist sector. Capital is indeed very necessary to increase labour productivity and skill. It is necessary to use fixed capital to its fullest possible extent. Marx rightly observes that the real barrier to capitalist development is capital itself.

Very often, the creation of social utility or social production is hampered by the shameless profit motive of the capitalists. The coordination of the different branches of the economy is not done, and the capitalist process of growth is, therefore, punctuated by crisis.

Marx was careful enough to pinpoint the lopsided nature of capitalist development. Marx's theory of capitalist development amply demonstrates the fact that capital-deepening process of development not only leads to a fall in the rate of profit via increasing organic composition of capital, but also to the proliferation of unemployment of labour as shown in Figure 2.1.

Figure 2.1 Unemployment of Labour

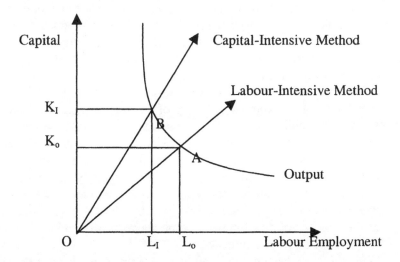

From the above figure, it becomes clear that society's stock of labour can be absorbed if labour-intensive method of production is adopted, but a shift to a capital-intensive method of production will create unemployment of labour to the extent of $L_1 L_o$. Thus, capitalist development via centralisation of capital leads to proletarianisation and immiserisation of the working class.

The analysis of the growth of reserve army of labour forms are indeed a part and parcel of Marx's theory of capitalist development, and goes a long way in explaining the phenomenon of dwindling effective demand which later became the heart of Keynesian analysis.

Towards a Critical Appraisal

Marx's ideas on development and underdevelopment have been castigated in various ways. *Firstly*, in response to Marx's discussion on the Asiatic mode of production, many Marxist scholars have rejected Marx's generalisation of the absence of private property in land in Asiatic societies. Marx's generalisation was counter-factual. However, Marx later recognised the private property in land. Marx could not analyse in detail as to how industrialisation could take place with western capital, particularly when colonial drain continued from the Asiatic countries. He did not explain as to how the primitive accumulation of capital, which helped the development of capitalism in Europe, could take place in Asiatic societies.

A.I. Chicherov has argued that Asiatic mode of production, contrary to Marx's belief, is not really a hindrance to the development of industrial capitalism in India and that capitalism could have developed in India but for the retarding impact of imperialism.[23]

The apparent specificity of the AMP seems to undermine the general formulation of Marxian stage theory of development, and in particular, the general applicability of dialectical materialism and class struggle. For these reasons, AMP was rejected as a Marxian tool of analysis in a conference held at Leningrad in 1931 under the direction of Stalin. However, after de-stalinisation since mid-fifties, the concept has again been recognised.[24]

Secondly, Marx' stage theory of development can be criticised on the grounds that the order of the stages given by Marx is not inevitable and that for the purpose of development, some stages can be skipped over. This is borne out by historical evidence.

Thirdly, it has been pointed out by critics that capitalist development does not necessarily lead to proletarianisation. Pranab Bardhan's empirical study of Indian agro-climatic regions shows that areas of high degree of proletarianisation are not technically progressive, and capital accumulation has taken place more impressively in areas where the proportion of wage labour is relatively low.[25] Bardhan has also challenged the empirical veracity of Marx's statement that institutions like share-cropping are fetters on development in poor agricultural countries. Bardhan argues that in the case of market failure and things like that, share-cropping is good, and certainly not as bad as Marx contemplates it to be.[26]

Fourthly, Marx's analysis of surplus extraction approach having its deleterious effect on capital accumulation has also been challenged. An analysis made by Amit Bhaduri shows that surplus extraction by rentier capital may drive the poor peasants in the exchange relations like the distress-selling of land and so on, raising the index of commercialisation but without having any effect on capital accumulation.[27]

Lastly, Marx's assertion that the negative role of state is responsible for the backwardness of Asiatic countries can also not be regarded as wholly true.[28]

But despite these points of criticism, it must be admitted that Marx was the earliest propounder of *stage theory* of development for which W.W. Rostow has expressed indirectly his indebtedness to Marx. Marx was aware of the possibility of disproportionality in development in the event of disequilibrium between saving and investment, and also between consumption and investment. He was also aware of the properties of balanced growth which Marx propounded in his analysis of reproduction schema.

Marx has rightly recognised the crucial importance of capital accumulation and technology in the process of development. Needless to say, inadequacy of availability of these two factors has been mainly responsible for the sluggish development of poor countries of our times.

Marxian prescription that more and more investment must be concentrated in the surplus-generating sector has remained a celebrated investment criterion for the developing countries.[29] In India, Mahalanobis model recommended the allocation of more and more resources to capital goods sector so that capital base could be created and surplus could be generated for economic development.

As a matter of fact, the mainstream development economics of our times owes a good deal to Marx and Marxists. The Marxian concepts like unequal exchange, uneven development, surplus extraction, dependency and dialectic nature of development are very central to the modern development economics.[30] Marxian analysis provides an apparatus of thought, and its essential contents can be used for analysing a wide range of problems of developing countries. Marxian concepts and tools may be more or less applicable in our context much the same way as Malthusian, Marshallian and Keynesian concepts. What is more important is not so much the written words of Marx, but the spirit of his analysis. The message of his analysis of development and underdevelopment has some universal appeal to keep it alive for posterity.

Notes

1. For the purpose of exposition here, no nuance is made between *growth and development*, although I do not deny such a nuance to exist.
2. The theory of evolution is discussed by Marx in his *German Ideology*, and *A Critique of Political Economy, inter alia.*
3. Karl Marx, *Preface, 1859.*
4. See, Tom Bottomore, *A Dictionary of Marxist Thought*, Oxford University Press, London, 1983, p. 398.
5. Eric Hobsbawm, "Introduction to Karl Marx", in *Pre-Capitalist Economic Formation*, Lawrence & Wishart, 1964.
6. Ibid., p. 12.
7. See, M. C. Howard and J. E. King, *The Political Economy of Marx*, Longmans, London, 1975, p. 4.
8. Karl Marx, *Critique*, p. 21.
9. Leon Trotsky, *The History of the Russian Revolution* (Translated by Max Eastman), Victor Gllancz, 1934, Vol. I, Ch. I.
10. See, among others, *Das Kapital, Introduction to the Critique of Political Economy*, British Rules in India" and *Grundrisse.*
11. Karl Marx, "British Rule in India", *New York Daily Times*, 25 June, 1853 and "Future Results of British Rule in India", *New York Daily Tribune*, 22 July 1853.
12. V. I. Pavlov, *Historical Premises of India's Transition to Capitalism*, Nanka Publishing House, Moscow, 1978.
13. Tapan Roychowdhury, "The Asiatic Mode of Production and India's Foreign Trade in the 17th Century: A Theoretical Exercise", *Essays in Honour of Professor S.C. Sarkar*, People's Publishing House, Delhi, 1976.
14. See, Irfan Habib, "Problems of Marxist Historical Analysis", *Enquiry*, Monsoon, 1969.
15. See, for details, Kenzo Mohri, "Marx and Underdevelopment", *Monthly Review*, April, 1979 and S.K. Ghosh, "Marx on India", *Monthly Review*, January 1984.
16. Karl Marx, *Capital*, Vol. I, Ch. 15.
17. See, V. Lenin, *Imperialism: The Highest Stage of Capitalism*, Collected Works, Moscow, 1964.
18. Paul Samuelson, "Wages and Interest: A Modern Discussion of Marxian Economic Models", *American Economic Review*, Vol. 47, 1957.
19. Jon Elster, "The Theory of Combined and Uneven Development: A Critique", in John Roemer (ed.), *Analytical Marxism*, Cambridge University Press, Cambridge, 1986, p. 62.
20. Donald J. Harris, "On Marx's Schema of Reproduction and Accumulation", *Journal of Political Economy*, Vol. 85, 1972.
21. Leon Trotsky, *Op. Cit.*
22. Karl Marx, *Capital*, Vol. III.
23. A. I. Chicherov, *India: Economic Development from Sixteenth to Eighteenth Centuries*, Nanka Publishing House, Moscow, 1971.
24. See, Tom Bottomore, *A Dictionary of Marxist Thought*, Oxford University Press, London, 1983.
25. Pranab K. Bardhan, "Agrarian Class Formation in India", *Journal of Peasant Studies*, Vol. X, No. 1, 1982.

26. Ibid.
27. Amit Bhaduri, *The Economic Structure of Backward Agriculture*, Academic Press, London, 1983.
28. Pranab K. Bardhan, "Marxist Ideas in Development Economics: An Evaluation", in John Roemer (ed.), *Analytical Marxism*, Cambridge University Press, Cambridge, 1986, pp. 64-77.
29. This criterion has also been suggested by W. Galenson and H. Lefibenstein, see, W. Galenson and H. Leibenstein, "Investment Criteria, Productivity and Economic Growth, *Quarterly Journal of Economics*, August, 1955.
30. Pranab K. Bardhan, "Marxist Ideas in Development Economics: An Evaluation", in John Roemer (ed.), *Op. Cit.*, pp. 64-77.

3 Paul Baran's Analysis of Economic Backwardness and Economic Growth

Paul Baran is one of the earliest writers to have given a political economic explanation of economic backwardness and economic growth. He is perhaps the first writer to develop the theory of dependency on the Marxist tradition. His theory is basically the Marxist theory of economic development, as it originated in Marx's own writing on the origins, development and contradictions of capitalism.[1] Baran expresses his ideas at three main places in his article, namely, "On the Political Economy of Backwardness", *The Manchester School* (January 1952), in his book, *The Political Economy of Growth*, Monthly Review Press (1957) and in the book that he wrote with Paul M. Sweezy on *Monopoly Capital;* Monthly Review Press (1966). In the following pages, I will discuss the central theme of Baran's analysis of development and underdevelopment.

Essential Features of Paul Baran's Analysis

Paul Baran observes that the analysis of development and underdevelopment comes within the jurisdiction of political economy. This is evident from the fact that the classical economists were concerned primarily with the question of economic backwardness and economic growth. As a matter of fact, Adam Smith's *Wealth of Nations* can be regarded as a book on economic development.

Baran's analysis considers economic questions as inseparable from social, political and ideological ones; and he regards the world as a totality of developed and backward capitalist countries and socialist countries which all interrelate with one another.[2] Baran has discussed different types of economic relationship between developed and underdeveloped countries within the capitalist system. He has observed that while in the advanced countries, capitalism leads to stagnation or militarism or both, in the

28

underdeveloped countries, it strangles all efforts at economic development.[3] Baran is of the view that underdevelopment is rooted in the same earth as development; they are the common results of a world-wide process of capital accumulation. This idea of Baran had been partly implicit in the writings of Marx and other Marxist writers like Luxemburg and Hilferding.[4]

Baran observes that the capitalist mode of production during the later part of the eighteenth century and also during the entire nineteenth century was able to expand productivity and material welfare quite sufficiently in different parts of the world. But the material progress was spotty in time and was not also evenly distributed in space.[5] Most of the material gain was confined to the Western countries; it did not affect the less developed countries (LDCs). In other words, one type of country could not gather enormous surplus and became economically developed, and the other type of country could gather surplus; rather, their own surplus was taken away by the other type of countries who became later developed countries (DCs). Baran shows that neither development nor underdevelopment could be understood unless the global interdependence of these two types of countries are taken into account. Economic development in LDCs is profoundly inimical to the dominant interests of the DCs. In fact, the exploitation of the LDCs has played an important role in the development of Western capitalism.

The present-day LDCs, have no recourse to primary accumulation of capital which was available to the DCs of our times. Moreover, the LDCs today face some problems in the age of monopoly capitalism which the DCs did not face some two or three hundred years ago. The DCs and LDCs had to face two different types of situation, and whereas the DCs could grow, the LDCs could not.

In this connection, Paul Baran has defined growth as an increase of per capita material goods over time. This is a concept of quantitative growth. There are mainly three sources of economic growth. *Firstly*, growth may be achieved by fully utilising the unutilised resources like population, land, capital and so on. *Secondly*, growth can also be achieved by making some organisational changes. This involves the shifting of resources from less productive uses to more productive uses, and *Thirdly*, by providing a better technology and capital, growth can also be attained. It is clear by now that in order to have economic growth, it is necessary to have better technical knowledge and higher rate of growth of investment. Since these two factors are not sufficiently available in LDCs, these countries remain underdeveloped.

Economic growth essentially depends on the accumulation of *surplus* and its proper utilisation. Thus, it is necessary to properly analyse the question of surplus in this connection. According to Paul Baran, there are *three main types* of economic surplus. These are: *Actual Economic Surplus*, *Potential Economic Surplus*, and *Planned Economic Surplus*. Actual surplus is the difference between society's actual current output and its actual current consumption. The potential surplus is the difference between what the society could produce in a given natural and technological environment with the help of employable productive resources, and what might be regarded as the necessary consumption. Potential surplus is generally bigger than the actual surplus in a capitalist society. Planned surplus is the difference between the society's optimum output attainable in a historically given natural and technological situation obtainable in a planned economy and the optimal volume of consumption. Planned surplus is relevant in a planned economy under socialism. The nature of these three types of surplus is summarised in the following chart.

Typology of Surplus

Actual Surplus	**Potential Surplus**	**Planned Surplus**
Difference between what society currently produces and what it actually consumes	Difference between what society could produce and what it needs to consume	Difference between society's planned optimum production and planned optimal consumption
Can be realised without any organisational change	Can be realised by making some organisational changes	Can be realised only under planned regime.

As has been pointed out earlier, the realisation of potential surplus needs some organisational changes. The actual surplus is nothing but the current saving or capital accumulation. The optimum production and consumption are to be determined under the ideal conditions of a planned economy like socialism. Under socialism, economic surplus is not determined by the consideration of profit maximisation but by the stage of historical development and also by the degree of development of productive forces and the structure and growth of human needs. According to Baran, the really important concept is not the *actual economic surplus* but the *potential economic surplus*. The concept of potential economic surplus includes the consumption spending of the state and the unnecessary consumption of the workers and capitalist. Potential surplus is the surplus which could be used for economic development with a different organisational set-up. Baran asserts that potential surplus rises during the development of monopoly capitalism, as has been found from experience.

It should be noted that Baran's concept of surplus is different from Marx's concept of *surplus value*. Whereas Marx has analysed surplus value in relation to the ownership of means of production, Baran has analysed *surplus* in relation to consumption needs of the society.[6] However, the implication of Baran's analysis of surplus is very profound in the sense that it is linked in the explanation of development and underdevelopment. Baran argues that DCs paradoxically generate an ever-increasing surplus, while at the same time failing to provide the consumption and investment outlets required for its absorption.[7] The DCs impose a particular form of development on the colonies in which the economic surplus produced is appropriated by foreign firms and domestic comprador class to the detriment of the colonial countries. The loss of surplus from these countries has made them underdeveloped. According to Baran, the problem for the DCs is one of an overproduction of economic surplus, but for the developing countries, the problem is the lack of access to surplus for their economic development.[8]

LDCs are underdeveloped because they have lower production, and because the degree of utilisation of human and material resources has also been lower there. Underdevelopment and under-utilisation of resources go hand in hand. The capitalist frame-work that is existing there is responsible for the economic stagnation and archaic technology of these poor countries. The size of economic surplus in such countries is very low. This is not due to higher consumption but due to small scale production and exploitation by the capitalists. Moreover, these countries have low capital endowment, low productivity, low saving and rapid growth of population. Whatever capital LDCs receive from abroad, is designed to extract surplus from these countries by the foreign capitalists. Whenever an increased national income

31

takes place, it does not benefit the common people because of the system of skewed distribution.[9]

The introduction of capitalism in LDCs does not do much good but it does enormous harm to these countries by generating economic and social tensions which are inherent in the capitalist order. Such an order effectively disrupted whatever was left of the feudal system of the backward countries.[10] Capitalism substituted market contracts for the paternalistic relationships which existed in these countries in the past. Capitalism forced the LDCs to produce marketable raw materials for the DCs. Such countries also became the markets for the finished products of the DCs. In this way, the LDCs were linked with the vagaries of world capitalist markets. The imported capitalism superimposed some business ethics which resulted in exploitation, corruption and injustice. The new machines worked for their foreign owners and not for the benefit of the domestic population. The wealthy business people reaped immense profits but did not utilise them for productive purposes. What resulted was an amalgam combining the worst features of both feudalism and capitalism, and it blocked all possibilities of economic growth in LDCs.

In LDCs, the majority of the population depended on agriculture. But the share of surplus that accrued to the landowning class was not utilised for economic development. The surplus produced from agriculture was utilised in excess consumption. The landowning class spends huge amount of money for conspicious consumption on luxury articles, on servants, on entertainment and travels. The landed aristocracy does not spend money for the improvement of agriculture. The situation is still worse for the small farmers who cannot introduce modern technology for want of funds and also due to small size of land-holdings. This is the reason why Baran observed that the breaking down of large estates into small holdings will not be very helpful. This method cannot put an end to the stagnation of agriculture in backward countries. Land reforms may bring some benefits to the farmers, but in the long-run, such benefits will be wiped out as a result of an increase in population. An increase in population will necessitate further partitions of land holdings into smaller plots.

The induction of capitalism in the domestic economy destroys the rural handicrafts and cottage industries. And this leads to the dissolution of the pre-capitalist structure of the economy and it also disintegrates the natural self-sufficiency of the domestic economy. However, this is a general possibility. It may not be true for all types of underdeveloped countries. But one thing which becomes clear is that when foreign goods are imported from abroad, the possibility of domestic production of those goods is reduced, and the size of the market becomes limited.

The introduction of the monopolistic type of industry in the domestic economy of the dependent country puts an obstruction to the growth of industrial capitalism. In such a situation, the transition of capital from the sphere of circulation to the sphere of production becomes pretty difficult. Under such a situation, agricultural growth becomes stagnant, and structural unemployment becomes a reality. The basic point in the explanation of underdevelopment in the schema presented by Baran is that the economic surplus which is appropriated by the monopolistic firms is not utilised for the purpose of economic development and for increasing production. Economic surplus in dissipated by the monopolists in unproductive manners. Only a small amount is spent for the purchase of rent-bearing property, in speculation and in usury.

Baran has also pointed out that a large amount of money is sent abroad as hedges against the depreciation of the domestic currency or as nest eggs assuring their owners of suitable retreats in the case of social and political upheavals at home.[11] The foreign firms do not bother about capital formation in the underdeveloped countries. On the other hand, most of the foreign firms send their profits abroad from the country in which they are engaged in business. Sometimes the profits are sent to those countries abroad where the rate of return on investment is higher. Generally, the profits of one underdeveloped country are not sent to another underdeveloped country; but instead, the profits are sent from one underdeveloped country to a developed country in the form of investment. It has been rightly pointed out that the main effect of foreign capital on the development of underdeveloped countries lies in hardening and strengthening the swag of Merchant Capitalism which slows down and indeed prevents the transformation of Merchant Capitalism into Industrial Capitalism. Baran is of the opinion that unless Merchant Capitalism is transformed into Industrial Capitalism, there cannot be any economic development in the true sense of the term. This is also the view of Karl Marx.

Baran has observed that the main obstacle in the way of economic development in LDCs is the lack of proper utilisation of surplus. Another reason is the availability of a very low volume of surplus. Development cannot be initiated because there is the deficiency of investment opportunities in such countries. This difficulty largely arises from the structure and the limitations of the existing effective demand simply because of low income. Most of the money out of low income is spent on food and other basic necessities of life. Only a small amount is left over for investment, which is inadequate. Moreover, it does not appear to be profitable to start major enterprises only for a small number of rich people. These people generally import the luxury goods of snob values from abroad. In such a case, there is no point in developing major industries at home. The limited demand for investment goods also precludes the building up of a machinery or equipment industry.[12] All this leaves the expansion of exportable raw material output as a major outlet for investment activities in LDCs.[13] However, there may be many difficulties in the matter of export. These are: uncertainty about foreign demand, prices and output of other countries which are competing. All this will sharply reduce the interest of the native capitalist in the business of export.

The most serious difficulties in the way of economic development in underdeveloped countries are the shortage of investible funds and the lack of investment opportunities. However, they represent two aspects of the same problem.[14] Moreover, investment in such countries is a new experience. Mostly, the new investments cannot be expected to reap external economies. The absence of external economies, the inadequacy of the economic milieu in LDCs constituted everywhere an important deterrent to investment in industrial projects. Investment really depends on some previous investment. Baran rightly says that large scale investment is predicated upon large-scale investment. Before any investment is made, there must be proper infrastructure. Moreover, the business people in LDCs are exposed to big businesses. Their financial resources are too small for ambitious projects, but they do not have the habit of entering into commitments. These people are not habituated in sinking funds in enterprises where profitability is unattractive and risk is high.

In the field of agriculture, the fallow lands can be brought to cultivation only after making considerable investment. Agriculture also requires a lot of innovations. But the peasants in LDCs are utterly unable to pay for such innovation. They do not have the financial ability to import costly equipment for the development of agriculture. Agriculture can be partly improved by the establishment of industries like fertilisers, electric power and so on. But in such countries, the prospect of industrial development is also limited. Monopolistic market structure, shortage of savings, lack of external economies and the divergence of social and private rationalities are the basic obstacles in the way of development of underdeveloped countries. These obstacles have to be considered against the background of the general feeling of uncertainty prevailing in backward areas.[15] Moreover, there are many types of inherent instability of the political and social order. Peasant uprisings, strikes and local guerrilla warfare from time to time are the grim reminders of the latent crisis in such countries. This type of climate is not congenial for making investment in long-term projects.

Baran has brought out four important popular fallacies which are cited while discussing obstacles to economic development.[16] *Firstly*, it is wrongly said that lack of entrepreneurial talent is one of the main obstacles in LDCs. According to Baran, this is not true. There are many good entrepreneurs in LDCs. *Secondly*, Baran says that it is not true to say that there is lack of capital in LDCs. He is of the opinion that potential surplus available in LDCs is quite large. *Thirdly*, Baran does not agree with the popular belief that population problem is a serious menace to economic development in LDCs. He believes that relative overpopulation can be judged only with reference to the means of production. Like Marx, Baran points out that overpopulation has to be considered only with reference to the means of production and employment. *Lastly*, Baran does not agree with the popular view that falling terms of trade are responsible for economic underdevelopment. If the prices of the domestic commodities rise, it will benefit only the foreign exporters who are operating in the domestic economy, and it will mean a transfer of larger amount of profit abroad by the foreign capitalists. An improved term of trade will not benefit the domestic economy.

According to Baran, underdevelopment is a condition which arises in the course of economic development. In this connection, Baran has illustrated the case of India which failed to develop because of its incorporation in the world capitalist system, and Japan succeeded in developing because of its isolation from the system.[17] The capitalist system has severely hampered all possibility of successful development in other parts of the underdeveloped world. Baran was of the view that the British, while enriching themselves, "....systematically destroyed all the fibres and foundations of Indian society....".[18] Baran proposed to demonstrate that these exploitative relationships and their consequence of persistent impoverishment epitomised the entire peripheral structure of world capitalism. In the same way, Paul Sweezy claimed that capitalist development inevitably produces development at one pole and underdevelopment at the other.

One can now summarise the basic arguments of Paul Baran for explaining the situation of underdevelopment.[19] The central point of Baran's analysis is that the main obstacle to the rapid growth of LDCs is the way in which their potential surplus is utilised. The size of the surplus does not matter so much. Baran argues that much of the potential economic surplus is not realised.

Secondly, much of the realised economic surplus is misused by those who appropriate it. A large part of the surplus is spent for maintaining unemployed labour and excess industrial capacity, and also in wasteful expenditure and in consumption stimulated by the international demonstration effect imposed by the multinational corporations. The wasteful and luxury expenditures are made by landlord and capitalist classes. These classes include moneylenders, landlords, and merchants. The state is also responsible for heavy expenditures on police and military forces. Apart from all these, much of the realised surplus goes out of these countries in the form of profit repatriation by foreign capitalists or service payments on the foreign debt, or as capital flight by the local elite who hold deposits overseas. *Finally*, if an underdeveloped country tries against all odds to overcome its underdevelopment, it is likely to find that its efforts are frustrated by the animosity of imperialism towards all genuine initiative at economic development on the part of the underdeveloped countries.[20] The Centre tries to keep the periphery under its firm control.

Drawing on the Marxist line of approach, Baran has shown that the penetration of capitalism into a feudal economy was an important obstacle to economic development. The local power structure and the foreign capitalists combined in a very palpable manner to fleece the people and the country. The surplus which could be utilised for development went out of the country. And the combination of local feudalism with capitalism blocked all possibilities for economic development.

What then is the way out? How can the underdeveloped countries be developed? In the final chapter of his book, Baran has discussed the possibilities of economic development of underdeveloped countries. Baran observes that it is essential first of all to have a social revolution, but this will inevitably encounter the hostility of the imperial power.[21] The establishment of a socialist planned economy is also essential for economic and social progress of underdeveloped countries. It is very necessary to mobilise the potential economic surplus of a country. A number of steps like the expropriation of foreign and domestic capitalists, land owners, elimination of capital drain, restriction of consumption, flight of capital to foreign countries and so on have to be applied. In this way, sufficient resources can be made available for the generation of new productive employment. Non-essential imports should also be banned and transfer of funds can be restricted. This will also be helpful for the mobilisation of resources for productive uses.

In a planned economy, there will be the growth of planned economic surplus. This can be equitably distributed among the population of the country in such a way that it leads to optimum social and material development of the country in the long run. In a socialist type of development, both agriculture and industry can be simultaneously developed. Regarding the method of development to be adopted, one has to remember the planned objectives of the country.

Agricultural development can be achieved by the use of improved seeds, improved methods of irrigation and also by improved usage of better inputs like fertilisers and so on. Substantial increase in productivity and output will depend on the possibility of introducing modern type of machinery, power and schemes of specialisation. It will be necessary to productively employ the unemployed and underemployed labour force of the country. For all these, a substantial amount of investment becomes essential.

A number of measures can be taken up by the government for overcoming economies backwardness.[22] *Firstly*, the government has to take up those lines of production which are not favoured by the private sector. The government has to start production and encourage competition where there is monopoly and restriction. *Secondly*, the state has to build-up the proper infrastructure for making further investment profitable. *Thirdly*, it is necessary to check the inflationary pressure through proper monetary and fiscal policies. *Fourthly*, a proper type of progressive taxation has to be introduced for not only controlling inflation but also for eliminating wasteful consumption and expenditure on non-essential activities. *Lastly,* the government needs to open technical schools for imparting skill and also for the growth of human capital formation. A proper system of education would be necessary for devising a right type of planning for economic development of an underdeveloped country.

It would be essential to properly control the foreign exchange resources of the country and to restrict the use of the limited supply of foreign exchange. Foreign aid has to be used with care because aid, like trade, may be very harmful at times for LDCs. The social and political climate of the country also needs to be drastically revamped in such a way that common people are benefited.

Critical Appraisal

Baran's analysis of economic backwardness and economic growth has remained very original and incisive. But it is not altogether free from blemishes. A number of criticisms can be levelled against Baran's analysis. *First*, Baran's theory as given in his *Monopoly Capital* (1966) which was written with Sweezy, is criticised principally because it departed from Marxist tradition, by utilising the concept of economic surplus rather than surplus value for an examination of advanced capitalist economies.[23] *Second*, it is practically very difficult to distinguish between his concepts of *potential surplus* and *planned surplus*. This is so because both these types of surpluses arise only after some necessary changes by the authority. And these changes are mostly done through some sort of planning, even if the country is not fully socialist in character. *Third*, Kaldor in his review of Baran's book (1957) said that the whole thesis of Baran hinges on the theory of distribution. But unfortunately, Baran has not given any discussion on the theory of distribution.[24] *Fourth*, Kaldor cast doubt on Baran's contention that monopoly capital in its mature stage led to a restriction of the rate of technical advance or to a slower growth of the purchasing power of the masses. *Fifth*, in his *Manchester School* paper (1952), Baran says that one of the causes of underdevelopment is low saving and high consumption.[25] This is not factually true in most of the underdeveloped countries. For instance, in a country like India, saving forms nearly 12 per cent of the national income and this is mostly contributed by the private sector.

Similarly, the consumption level of the poor people of these countries is not at all very high, although a small section of the population may be engaged in conspicuous consumption. *Sixth*, Baran did not sufficiently relate the facts of exploitation in the DCs and LDCs to the aid, trade and exchange relationships which he discusses in various parts of the book (1957). Indeed, he did not really have a theory of exploitation at all, though, of course, he never lost sight of the harmful effects of the capitalist system on large sections of the population of DCs, not to mention the LDCs.[26] According to R. B. Sutcliffe, this was an important theoretical omission when it comes to taking a political message from the economic situation which Baran elaborated.

Seventh, Baran did not consider the mechanism which causes the transition from actual to either potential or planned surplus, and *vice versa*. *Lastly*, in his suggestion for the removal of underdevelopment, Baran has advised for the establishment of a socialist society. However, socialism, as historical experience shows, is not a panacea. In many countries of our times, socialism has really failed.

However, all said and done, it must be admitted that Baran came equipped with a theory which saw underdevelopment in a global perspective and yet which could distinguish the position of the advanced country from that of an underdeveloped country.[27] His insights had given enormous influence on the ideas of the radical economists. His analysis of potential surplus has encouraged writers to explore the possibilities of self-reliant development and to investigate ways in which the surplus is generated and siphoned off to the rich countries. His analysis has given a new direction for the examination of the links among the domestic class structure, international dependency and capital accumulation.[28] Baran has made a definite contribution towards the development of Marxist theory.[29] Baran can really be considered as the father of dependency approach.[30]

Notes

1. R. B. Sutcliffe's "Introduction", in Paul A. Baran, *The Political Economy of Growth*, Penguin Books, England, 1957, pp. 63-64.
2. R. B. Sutcliffe, *Op. Cit.*, p. 70.
3. *Ibid.*, p. 100. In this connection, Baran says that capitalism can no longer be considered as a progressive force in the world. He does not see any significant chance of reforming capitalism.
4. Ibid., p. 99.
5. P. A. Baran, "On the Political Economy of Backwardness", *The Manchester School*, January, 1952, as given in C. K. Wilber (ed.), *Political Economy of Development and Underdevelopment*, Random House, USA, 1973, p. 8.
6. R. B. Sutcliffe, *Op. Cit.*, p. 91.
7. Tom Bottomore, *A Dictionary of Marxist Thought*, Oxford University Press, 1983, London, p. 498.
8. Paul Baran and Paul M. Sweezy, *Monopoly Capitalism*, Monthly Review Press, USA, 1966.
9. Paul A. Baran, "On the Political Economy of Backwardness", *Op. Cit.*, p. 82.
10. Ibid., p. 83.
11. Paul A. Baran, *The Political Economy of Growth*, 1957, *Op. Cit.*, p. 177. The domestic surplus in this way goes out of the country and the country becomes poorer and poorer.
12. Paul A. Baran, "On the Political Economy of Backwardness", *Op Cit.*, p. 87.
13. Loc. Cit.
14. Loc. Cit.
15. Ibid., p. 89.
16. See, Paul A. Baran, *The Political Economy of Growth*, *Op. Cit.*, Ch. VII.

17. *Op. Cit.*, Ch. V.
18. Ibid., *Ch. VIII.*
19. Theodore Morgan, *Economic Development*, Harper and Row, New York, 1975. Morgan has precisely summarised the measures suggested by Baran.
20. Henryk Szlajfer, "Economic Surplus and Surplus Value: An Attempt at Comparison", *Review of Radical Political Economics*, Spring 1983, p. 108.
21. See, N. Kaldor's Review of Baran's book in *American Economic Review*.
22. Paul A. Baran, "On the Political Economy of Backwardness", *The Manchester School*, January, 1952.
23. R. B. Sutcliffe, *Op. Cit.*, p. 90.
24. Ibid., p. 62.
25. Keith Griffin and John Gurley, *Op. Cit.*, p. 1112.
26. R. B. Sutcliffe, *Op. Cit.*, p. 99.
27. See, Gabriel Palma, "Dependency: A Formal Theory of Underdevelopment or a Methodology for the Analysis of Concrete Situations of Underdevelopment?", *World Development*, Vol. 6, 1978.
28. K. Griffin and John Gurley, "Radical Analyses of Imperialism. The Third World, and the Transition to Socialism: A Survey Article", *Journal of Economic Literature*, Sept., 1985, p. 1105.
29. John Gurley, "Economic Development: A Marxist View", as given in G.M. Meier, *Leading Issues in Economic Development*, Oxford University Press, London, 1984, p. 134.
30. A. G. Frank, *On Capitalist Underdevelopment*, Oxford University Press, 1977. This is true not only in the macro-context of the entire world economy, but also in the micro-context of a particular country.

4 Andre Gunder Frank's Analysis of Development of Underdevelopment

Gunder Frank has extended the analysis of Paul Baran. Baran, Frank and others of the dependency school argue that underdevelopment arose from the way the Third World was incorporated into an international economic and political system, dominated initially by Europe and later by the United States.[1] The main contributions of Frank are to be found in his five main books: *Capitalism and Underdevelopment in Latin America* (1967), *Latin America: Underdevelopment or Revolution* (1969), *On capitalist Underdevelopment* (1977), *Dependent Accumulation and Underdevelopment* (1979) and *Lumpen-bourgeoisie and Lumpen Development* (1972). After Baran, Frank is the most noted writer of the dependency school of thought. He carried and generalised Paul Baran's analysis to its logical conclusion. In the subsequent discussion, I will dwell on the main thesis of Andre Gunder Frank.

Major Tenets of Frank's Thesis on Development of Underdevelopment

Frank contended that capitalism had long ago entered every nook and corner of the satellite (periphery) world in such a way as to make global capitalism an integrated structure of metropoles and satellites that bound different countries, regions and rural-urban areas into dominant dependent relationshps.[2] A systematic transfer of economic surpluses continually occurred from the base of the world structure (periphery)to the metropolitan centres of the advance countries. The peripheries (satellites) are nothing but the underdeveloped regions of the world which are integrated with the world capitalist system. This process developed the metropoles and harmed the satellites which became underdeveloped. In a macro world structure, the developed capitalist countries (DCs), can be regarded as the metropolitan centres and the less developed countries (LDCs) can be regarded as the periphery. However, looked at from the micro structure of a particular underdeveloped country, its centre can be regarded as metropolitan and its peripheries like different rural areas and regions can be called satellites. Just as in a macro sense, a metropolitan centre can exploit its peripheries representing underdeveloped countries as a whole; similarly, a particular underdeveloped country can also amass a large amount of economic surplus by exploiting its own peripheries. In both the cases, the idea is to accumulate surplus. This leads to a temporary development of the metropolitan centre (towns and cities) of an underdevelopment country but such a centre is exploited by the macro metropolitan centre of the capitalist world. Hence, the developed metropolitan centre of a backward country is again reduced to an underdeveloped centre. On the other hand, by drawing the surplus from the satellite underdeveloped countries of the world, the DCs become more and more developed.

When a particular country is incorporated into the world capitalist structure, the economy of the former country shows all the signs and symptoms of the capitalist structure, including the contradictions inherent in capitalism. These contradictions generate development in the national metropolis and underdevelopment in the domestic periphery. But it should be noted that the national metropolis itself is a satellite of the world metropolis. Therefore, the development of the national metropolis really becomes limited and dependent. I can now briefly discuss some of the contradictions of capitalism.

The contradictions of capitalism emerge in the course of historical evolution of capitalism. In capitalism, economic surplus is produced by many, but it is appropriated by only a few. Moreover, under capitalism, there takes place a polarisation of the capitalist system into metropolitan centre and the periphery. More often than not, the periphery is exploited and the surplus is accumulated for the development of the metropolitan centre. Thus, *firstly*, the contradiction of capitalism manifests itself in a developed metropolitan centre and also an underdeveloped periphery. As a result of the monopoly structure of capitalism, the surplus generated in LDCs passes into the hands of the metropolis. The surplus which remains in the periphery, is misutilised and is spent away on various types of under-productive activities and speculation. *Secondly*, as pointed out earlier, capitalism leads to a contradictory division of the world into two parts – one part (metropolitan centre) becomes developed and the other part (satellite or periphery) becomes underdeveloped. In other words, one part of the system develops at the cost of the other part. This is not only true of the macro-structure of capitalism, it is equally true of the micro-structure of a particular capitalist country where a city develops at the cost of rural areas and regions. The metropolis-satellite contradiction runs in a chain-like order throughout the entire capitalist world. It works from above to down below the system. In every case, the surplus from the weaker part is extracted and transmitted through a series of metropolis-satellite links.[3]

Lastly, there is the contradiction of continuity in change. This implies that in spite of historical evolution of capitalism, its basic essential character has remained the same and the contradictions could not be eliminated. Frank has stressed the issue of continuity and similarity of dependency relations in the context of capitalism. He emphasises the similarities between economic structure of Cortex, Pizarro, Clive and Rhodes, and between those and the structures typified by the activity of multinational corporations.[4]

Frank points out that there are, in fact, no national economies at all. There are simply national sectors of the world capitalist economy. The LDCs are incorporated into the capitalist structure of DCs in such a way that the former simply become a sector of the latter.

Frank opines that the DCs were never underdeveloped, though they have been undeveloped. Underdevelopment, according to Frank, is not a historical stage of growth through which the DCs passed, but rather, it is the result of the historical development of the capitalist system. So long as the LDCs remain as a part of the world capitalist system, their underdevelopment will be accentuated. Development and Underdevelopment, in a sense, are the opposite sides of the same system because they are the product of single but dialectically contradictory economic structure of capitalism. They are not different stages within the same system. One and the same historical process of development of world capitalism has simultaneously produced and will continue to produce both economic development and structural underdevelopment.[5] The relationship between the metropolis and the periphery causes underdevelopment to the periphery. According to Frank, the relationship obstructs development and aggravates underdevelopment in a myriad of ways.[6]

In the model of development advanced by Gunder Frank, we can see *three* important planes in his analysis.[7] In the first plane, he shows that Latin American Countries have been inducted into the world economy since the early colonial era. In the second plane, he shows that such countries have become capitalised economies by their incorporation into the world economic system. In the third plane, he has demonstrated that there is a metropolis-satellite chain. Surplus is drawn away from the periphery by the centre, and as a result of that, the periphery is impoverished and the metropolitan centre is enriched. In the words of Frank: "....If it is satellite status which generates underdevelopment, then a weaker or lesser degree of metropolis, satellite relations may generate less deep structural under-development and/or allow for more possibility of local development....".[8]

Gunder Frank observes that a theory of underdevelopment should be able to "....explain the causes and the phenomena which have been brought about, and which maintain and generate the stagnation of Latin America and its distorted development....". The analysis of underdevelopment, according to him, should be based on historical experience and realistic approach with reference to the Latin American countries.[9] These countries were incorporated into the world capitalist system since long. Frank was pragmatic enough to point out that the same analysis which is applicable to Latin American countries, must also be applicable to other LDCs. The problems of Latin American and other LDCs are similar in many respects, and they are essentially structural in nature which cannot be solved by the planning process or through foreign aid and assistance. Once the LDCs were integrated with the world capitalist system and started participating in the game of trade, their socio-economic and political structure were entirely distorted and they acquired the nature of a typical underdeveloped country having a typical export economy. Since these countries are integrated with the world capitalist system, the laws and contradictions of capitalism creep into these LDCs and they help the development of underdevelopment.

Gunder Frank maintains that underdevelopment is not something original or traditional and that neither the past nor the present of the underdeveloped countries resembles in any important respect the past of the now developed countries.[10] Contemporary underdevelopment is mainly the historical product of past and continuing economic and other relations between the satellite underdeveloped and the now developed metropolitan countries. These relations are an essential part of the structure and development of the capitalist system on a world scale.[11] It is a wrong notion that development of LDCs must and will be generated by diffusing capital, institutions and values to them from the DCs. On the contrary, in LDCs, economic development can occur only independently of most of the capitalist relationship.

The hypothesis that there is dual society in LDCs – one modern and developed and the other traditional and underdeveloped, is a false hypothesis. It is not true to say that one part of the society is modern because of its relation with the capitalist system and the other part is not modern because it is not related to the capital system. If such a hypothesis is acted upon, it will only perpetuate and intensify the very conditions of underdevelopment which LDCs have been trying to remove. Capitalism has entered even the most isolated sector of the underdeveloped world in the past centuries. The present state of underdevelopment of Latin America is the result of its centuries-long participation in the process of world capitalist development. At some stage, monopolistic relation was introduced in Latin America, particularly in Chile. Chile has become increasingly marked by the economic, social and political structure of satellite underdevelopment. This development of underdevelopment continues today in Chile and also in Brazil.[12]

Frank upholds that underdevelopment is not due to the survival of archaic institution and the existence of capital shortage in LDCs that have remained isolated. On the contrary, underdevelopment is generated by the same historical process which generated economic development, i.e. the development of capitalism itself. Several hypotheses have been framed by Gunder Frank in connection with his thesis on development of underdevelopment. His *first* hypothesis is that within the world-embracing metropolis-satellite structure, the metropoles tend to develop and satellites tend to underdevelop. *Second* hypothesis states that the satellites experience their greatest economic development if and when their ties to their metropolis are weakest. This hypothesis seems to be confirmed by two kinds of relative isolation that Latin America has experienced in the course of its history. The classic case of industrialisation through non-participation as a satellite in the capitalist system is the case of Japan after the Meiji Restoration. Since Japan was not satellised; it did not have its development structurally limited as other countries which were satellised. The *third* hypothesis is that the regions which are the most underdeveloped and feudal-seeming today are the ones which had the closest ties to the metropolis in the past. This hypothesis contradicts the general belief that the source of a region's underdevelopment is its isolation from the capitalist world. Frank's *fourth* hypothesis is that "....the greater the wealth that was available for exploitation in the past, the poorer and more underdeveloped the region today; and the poorer the region was as a colony, the richer and more developed it is today....".[13]

The above hypotheses suggest that the global extension and unity of the capitalist system, its monopoly structure and uneven development throughout its history, and the resulting commercial rather than industrial capitalism in LDCs deserve much more attention than they have received in the past.[14]

Frank observes that the character and nature of change in a given society are defined through the market relations. For Frank, the problem of the origins of capitalism comes down to the origins of expanding world markets and not to the emergence of a system of free wage labour.[15] He developed a circular concept of capitalism in terms of its exchange relations. He has not given importance to the study of class relations in his analysis of development and underdevelopment. Frank has based his analysis on the premise that unequal market relationships within the capitalist economy and domestic economy produce development and underdevelopment on the international and national levels. Participation in trade with the capitalist world is responsible for the underdevelopment and a system which is producing output for the international market is a capitalist system.

In LDCs, the export sector has been an important source of monopoly power. This sector is mainly controlled by the foreigners. The foreigners also control many other associated fields like transport, insurance and so on. And such controls ultimately dominate the political and military spheres of the domestic economy. Once involved in the dependency relationship, the LDCs became permanently incapable of moving out of the structure of dependence and underdevelopment. As a matter of fact, the pre-existing societies were entirely and completely transformed and became dependent on the capitalist system. In the process of underdevelopment of LDCs, the domestic bourgeoisie not only extracts surplus from the periphery, he is also interested in the continuance of foreign domination. But a time comes when the dependent bourgeoisie is not more capable of enhancing capitalist development. The important point made by Frank is that when capitalism is engulfing the whole world, it is not proper to consider any region or sector as feudal or non-capitalist. It is capitalism everywhere.[16]

In the case of Latin America, the structure that emerged can be called colonial capitalism but not feudalism. The countryside was to some extent feudal, but the cities were capitalist. Frank maintains that Brazilian agriculture was fully integrated into the capitalist system. The manifestations of capitalism are different in DCs and LDCs, but it does not imply that development is caused by capitalism and underdevelopment is caused by feudalism. Many people wrongly mistake metropolis-satellite polarisation of the capitalist society and the monopoly concentration in LDCs as examples of feudalism. The existence of subsistence farming or family workshops and artisans does not indicate the existence of feudalism. According to Frank, the underdevelopment of agriculture is not due to the existence of feudalism but because of its complete integration with the world capitalist system.

Frank observes that with the passage of time, the structure of dependence has remained more or less the same but the basis of monopoly within the capitalist system has changed over time. For instance, in the present century, the basis of metropolitan monopoly has more and more turned towards technology and its diffusion to LDCs. The LDCs cannot really innovate these technologies. They have to depend on the technology transfer from the DCs; but these imported technologies are not suitable to LDCs. The LDCs for no fault of their own, experience balance of payments deficits. Then, they have to take more foreign loans and assistance. Balance of payments deficit, resultant devaluation and increased money supply lead to inflation, which distort the whole situation in LDCs. In this way, the LDCs are involved in a trap of dependent structure. Very little capital is invested by the foreigners in domestic economies. Most of the capital is nothing but the profit earned from less developed countries. But the returns from these investments go to the metropolis.

In many ways, the surplus of the domestic economy is continuously drained out of the domestic economy in connivance with the national bourgeoisie. In a chain-like system of exploitation, the metropolitan centre of the advanced country exploits the national bourgeoisie who in turn also exploits the people of the domestic economy who are living in the periphery. Development at the core requires underdevelopment in the periphery. In such a system of dependence, the requirement of technology, finance, imports and things like that are determined by the metropolitan centre. Frank rightly says that American influence has considerably increased over Brazil, so much so that Brazilian imports requirements are determined by the United States. In this way, the metropolitan centre wields considerable control and influence over the income and resources of the less developed countries.

The capitalist metropolis-satellite structure is maintained by foreign capitalists, big domestic capitalists and rich land-owning classes. The domestic powerful interest group promotes policies producing underdevelopment of the domestic economy. Thus, it can be seen that Brazil could not be made fully independent even after the achievement of political independence, as the rulers were interested in maintaining the satellite status of Brazil. The closer the ties between the satellite and the metropolis, the closer becomes the national bourgeoisie link with the metropolis. Because of this link, the domestic economy cannot fully develop. The state also becomes an instrument of the domestic bourgeoisie. Frank has observed that in a country like Latin America, the immediate enemy of national liberation is the native bourgeoisie. So long as the system cannot be changed, there is no possibility of development.

Then, how can there be development of these backward countries? How to solve their problem of underdevelopment? Frank maintains that the only alternative which is possible is that of breaking completely with metropolis-satellite network through the socialist revolution.[17] But the weakening of the satellite-metropolis network can only take place for reasons external to the satellite economies which may be transient in character. There is no real possibility of sustained development within the system. Another possibility is the withdrawal by the industrial capitalist countries from the LDCs. In any case, it is necessary to snap the ties and linkages with the metropolitan country. Dissolution of capitalism can be very helpful for the economic development of LDCs. A movement for the complete liberation of the backward country has to be started before any attempt is made for the economic development of the country. But such a step would be bold and would require the sacrifice of men and materials. Having outlined the major tenets of Gunder Frank's main thesis on development and underdevelopment, I am now in a position to summarise the basic points of Frank by way of conclusion.

Gunder Frank has shown that underdevelopment is not an inherent defect of a country. It is a product of colonialism. The capitalism existing in the peripheries did not evolve from feudalism or pre-capitalist mode of production. Capitalist mode of production was rather imposed from outside. Such a type of implanted capitalism did not help the development of satellite countries. On the other hand, it made them more dependent and backward. As a matter of fact, world capitalism has produced development and underdevelopment at the same time. Certain contradictions of capitalism are responsible for this type of situation. Capitalism has spread in LDCs and has created a chain of exploitative metropolis-satellite relationship which has worked in favour of DCs and against the LDCs.

The stronger the metropolis-satellite relationship, the greater is the extent of underdevelopment in the satellite countries, and the weaker the relationship, the lesser is the extent of underdevelopment. Economic development has taken place only when the ties with the metropolis were temporarily weakened due to wars, depressions and other problems. The metropolis-satellite relations also exist between the relatively advanced capital city and the oppressed backward hinterland. These relations may be national or international. Nationally (from micro point of view), such relations can create sub-metropolis within a domestic economy which also has satellite rural and backward regions. Whether it is national or international, the relationship is meant for accumulating the surplus from the weaker national/international periphery. Frank has shown that the regions presently most underdeveloped are those that were most tightly linked to the metropolis in the past.[18]

The national bourgeoisie is helping the imperialist power to perpetuate domestic underdevelopment. This is very much observable in the Latin American countries which have not yet been developed even after attaining political independence. The surplus from LDCs is still now being siphoned off to DCs through various ways and means devised by multinational corporations and international organisations. Once a country is integrated with the world capitalist system, there would be gradual development of underdevelopment. And the LDCs are forced to become the suppliers of raw material for the DCs. The process blocks the industrial development of primary producing countries. The export orientations and foreign dominance over these countries has limited the growth of their domestic market and the establishment of basic national industries for their own development.

According to Gunder Frank, the countries in Asia, Africa and Latin America have remained underdeveloped through their contacts with the DCs. Their colonial status shaped the course of their economic history. They became exporters of primary products and importers of finished products. As a consequence, their structure of production and consumption became dislocated. The colonial trade pattern became a retarding force because this prevented merchant capital from being converted into industrial capital. The growth process of these economies became aborted. In this context, Frank illustrated the case of Latin America. In the sixteenth century, Spanish and Portuguese colonies were so completely integrated with the world capitalist system that they did not get any opportunity of achieving their own economic development.[19] They became satellites of the

49

Western metropolis. They were exploited and the surplus went for the development of the metropolis. This process, as Frank believes, is responsible for economic underdevelopment of many backward nations. Japan is an exception because it was not integrated with capitalist system. But the underdevelopment of Africa, Mexico and India was due to their integration with the world capitalist system.

Is there any hope for these backward countries? Frank advises them to break away from the capitalist system and turn towards socialist system. Moreover, internally, it is necessary to overthrow the bourgeoisie who are in collusion with the imperialist foreign power and start a socialist liberation movement by cutting all connections with the industrial capitalist countries.

From what has already been discussed, it becomes clear that Frank's analysis of underdevelopment and development involves macro-structures of metropolitan-periphery relations. While these structures happen to generate underdevelopment in backward countries, they correspondingly produce development for the DCs. The micro-structure relates to the structure of a backward country with periphery (p) and metropolis (m). A backward state centre (m) is a periphery of world capitalism. Within the micro-system of a country, surplus is extracted from the rural and regional periphery (p) and is sent to the state centre (m). Through loss of surplus, the periphery of a micro-state becomes underdeveloped, but its centre becomes comparatively developed. But ultimately, when the surplus of the state centre (m) is extracted from the world metropolis (M), then the state centre (m) becomes underdeveloped.

Frank's Micro-Macro Structures of Underdevelopment and Development

Micro-Structure of Development/Underdevelopment	Macro-Structure of Development/Underdevelopment
Relates to the structure of a backward country having periphery (p) and metropolis (m)	Relates to the structure of Capitalist world having its peripheries (P) and metropolis (M). The peripheries are nothing but the metropolis (M) of so many backward countries
A backward state centre (m) is a periphery of world capitalism	Metropolis of world capitalism is not a periphery of anybody or anything

Within the micro-system of a country, surplus is extracted from (p) and sent to (m)	Within the macro-structure of capitalist world, surplus is extracted from all dependent colonies/state centres (m), and it goes to the metropolis (M)
Through loss of surplus, (p) becomes underdeveloped, and (m) becomes comparatively developed	No surplus is lost, but it is gained from all dependent colonies/states Hence, (M) becomes developed
When surplus is extracted from the state metropolis (m) by the world metropolis (M), (m) becomes underdeveloped	There is no mechanism/agent to extract the surplus of macro-metropolitan centre (M)
Thus, both (p) and (m) become underdeveloped through macro structural exploitation	No exploitation is possible by the micro-structure. Macro-centre (M) develops uninterruptedly
Macro capitalist structure unfavourably influences the micro-structure of a backward country and produces underdevelopment in LDCs	Micro-structure of LDCs helps the development of the macro-structure in DCs

Thus, in course of time, both (p) and (m) become underdeveloped. Macro-capitalist structure unfavourably influences the micro-structure of a backward country. Macro-structure relates to the capitalist world having its peripheries (P) and metropolis (M). The peripheries are the LDCs where-from (M) draws away surplus which is utilised for the development of the capitalist economy at the centre. The macro-structure cannot be unfavourably influenced by the micro-structure. In other words, no surplus is lost from the macro-centre but it gains from all dependent colonies/states, and hence, it becomes developed at the cost of the LDCs. The structural schema of Frank's thesis is presented in the earlier Chart.

Critical Appraisal

Gunder Frank's work has been subjected to severe criticism from various directions. In what follows, I will briefly discuss some of the crucial criticisms against Frank's thesis.

First, Laclau argues that the defining characteristic of capitalism has to be located in the sphere of production.[20] Merely the existence or absence of a substantial market does not imply capitalism or feudalism respectively. Frank has not given emphasis on the production relations but has instead put emphasis on exchange relations. It is necessary to distinguish between capital in the sphere of exchange and capital in the sphere of production because the first does not automatically imply the second. M. B. Brown has also supported Laclau's view that Frank's analysis is un-Marxist because it emphasises exchange-relations in the world market rather than production relations.[21]

Second, Frank has neglected the specificities of internal mode of production and class structure of the periphery and their impact. He wrongly makes market or trade as the determining factor in class formation. Frank did not attempt to integrate an internal class structure into his analysis of underdevelopment. However, it should be noted that development of underdevelopment is actually rooted in the class structure of production. Frank did deal with class in his later analysis but he only treated it as a phenomenon directly derived from the needs of profit maximisation, i.e. as determined by the market and in relation to the needs of national and international metropolis. Frank did not specify the particular historically developed class structure and did not take into consideration labour productivity which is very crucial in any analysis of development and underdevelopment. It is also pointed out that Frank has ignored the role of state and its relations to class struggle and class alliances.

Third, Frank has used the concept of capitalism in a sense which is erroneous from a Marxist point of view and which is useless for his central proposition that wants to demonstrate that a bourgeois revolution in the periphery is impossible.[22] In this connection, Laclau concludes that Frank has not made any new contribution. He has left the analysis where it was.[23]

Fourth, in Frank's analysis, there is an attempt to have a mechanical determination of internal structure by the external structure. This has dominated his idea to construct a model to explain the mechanism through which the expropriation of surplus takes place.[24]

Fifth, Frank has not described the nature of the relations of dependence which keeps on changing along with changes in economic structures of DCs: the structures may be mercantilism, capitalism or imperialism. Each has its own nature of dependent relationship. According to Laclau, Frank's error follows from confusing the two concepts of capitalist mode of production and participating in world capitalist system.[25] Frank thought that the colonial economies were capitalist, but within the system of world capitalism, they had a dependent and subordinate status. Frank could not satisfactorily define the distance between exchange and production relations, and confused between the integration of a given area into a world market dominated by capitalism and the local installation of the capitalist mode of production.

Sixth, Frank's assertion that Latin America was capitalist from the time of the *Conquest*, has given rise to a number of theoretical problems, Sternberg argues that Frank's assertion does not tally with Marx's historical analysis of the times.[26]

Seventh, Frank has observed that Latin American countries and other developing countries including India were capitalist in nature. As for India, it has been pointed out by critics that Indian agriculture was feudal rather than capitalist.[27] The penetration of money and commerce is not necessarily an index of the growth of capitalist production relations. Simple exploitation of surplus does not mean capitalism, as Frank thinks. Feudalism is understood to be a closed or subsistence economy. Frank completely does away with the concept of production relations in his definitions of capitalism and feudalism. Frank is wrong in thinking that production for profit in the market is sufficient signal of capitalism and that trade relations are absent in feudalism. Frank's view that all peripheral countries were capitalists is not correct.

Eighth, Frank has shown how advanced countries have exploited the peripheral countries, but he has not explained why certain nations needed the underdevelopment of other nations for their own process of expansion.

Ninth, Frank's theory of underdevelopment does not seem to be empirically correct. For instance, as Brown pointed out, India and Egypt have not been able to develop so well industrially as some other LDCs, in spite of their being politically independent. Moreover, industrial production has increased per head in many countries but agricultural production has stagnated. Industrial development in Asia, Africa and Latin America does not empirically support Frank's main thesis that there is a continuous flow of wealth from periphery to the metropolis.

Tenth, Bill Warren has also observed that imperialist penetration has produced many advantages for the LDCs rather than producing underdevelopment.[28] Similarly, Alec Nove has pointed out that underdevelopment is not caused by the penetration of capitalism in LDCs.[29] According to Alec Nove, Frank spoils his case by overstatement. Nove says that underdevelopment of Zambia, Saudi Arabia and Ceylon is not caused by capitalism. According to him, many countries are underdeveloped because they are not exploited by the DCs. Even Russia had to borrow heavily from the Western countries for the development of its railways and other industries. None observes that capitalism need not be blamed for underdevelopment. Shanghai and Manchuria dominated by foreigners were developed. Underdevelopment of China was due to many factors like political paralysis, internal disorder and so on rather than imperialist penetration.

Eleventh, Frank's attitude to trade seems to suggest that the sale of some products to the western world is a cause of underdevelopment. This is really not so. Frank's diagnosis that capitalism is responsible for protection in DCs and free trade in LDCs is wrong.

Twelfth, according to some, when a backward country is integrated with a developed country, the productivity of labour in the former country must increase. However, this has not been the case in LDCs. This phenomenon cannot be explained by Frank's thesis.

Lastly, Frank proposes a complete break with capitalism and a revolution for socialism. This contradicts the laws of motion of capitalism because in that case the revolution does not depend on the development of capitalism but it would be something unnatural imposition from outside. Moreover, socialism is not the panacea for all evils. Even under socialism, there may be all the demerits of capitalism, as the experience of many socialist countries shows.

However, in spite of the above points of criticism, it must be conceded that after Baran, the most elaborate work on dependency theory has been performed by Gunder Frank. The value of Frank's analysis lies in his magisterial critique of the supposedly dual structure of peripheral societies.[30] Frank shows clearly that the different sectors of the economies in question are and have been since very early in their colonial history linked closely to the world economy. He has correctly brought out the fact that capitalist integration has not automatically brought about capitalist development in LDCs. Laclau has also agreed with Frank's criticism of the dualist thesis in LDCs. Frank's direct contribution to the understanding of the process of Latin American development is limited to his critique of the dualistic model. However, there are considerable indirect contributions of Frank's analysis. In 1978, Frank incorporated into his analysis the issue of internal class structure; according to this, underdevelopment is the result of exploitation of the colonial and class structures.[31] However, it is pointed out by Brenner that Frank has not been successful in his attempt in this direction.[32] But all said and done, one needs to remember that Frank's work has inspired a significant quantity of research in many disciplines concerning development and underdevelopment, particularly in the sociology of development.[33]

Notes

1. G. Palma, "Dependency: A Formal Theory of Underdevelopment or a Methodology for the Analysis of Concrete Situation of Underdevelopment?", *World Development*, Vol. 6, as given in G. Meier, *Op Cit.*, p. 141.
2. A. G. Frank, *Latin America: Underdevelopment or Revolution*, Monthly Review Press, USA, 1969.
3. A. G. Frank, *Capitalism and Underdevelopment in Latin America*, Monthly Review Press, USA, 1967.
4. G. Palma, *Op. Cit.*, p. 139.
5. A. G. Frank, *Capitalism and Underdevelopment in Latin America, Op. Cit*, p. 11.
6. Ibid. This is also true for all the other LDCs.
7. A. G. Frank, "The Development of Underdevelopment", *Monthly Review*, Sept., 1966, as given in C. K. Wilber (ed.), *Political Economy of Development and Underdevelopment*, Random House, USA, 1973, p. 95.
8. Loc Cit.
9. A. G. Frank, *Ibid.*, p. 97.
10. A.G. Frank *Lumpenbourgeoisie and Lumpendevelopment*, Monthly Review Press, USA, 1972, p. 19.
11. A. G. Frank, "The Development of Underdevelopment", *Op. Cit.*, p. 103.
12. G. Palma, *Op. Cit.*, p. 140.
13. A. G. Frank, *On Capitalist Underdevelopment, Op. Cit.*, pp. 97-98. The popular belief that there is feudalism in LDCs is challenged by Gunder Frank.
14. A. G. Frank, *On Capitalist Underdevelopment, Op. Cit.*, p. 103.
15. A. G. Frank, *Latin America: Underdevelopment or Revolution*, Monthly Review Press, 1969, pp. 9-13.
16. A. G. Frank, *On Capitalist Underdevelopment*, Oxford University Press, Bombay, 1975, p. 3.
17. E. Laclau, "Feudalism and Capitalism in Latin America", *New Left Review*, May-June 1971, pp. 19-38.
18. M. B. Brown, *The Economics of Imperialism*, Penguin Books, London, 1976.
19. G. Palma, *Op. Cit.*, p. 141.
20. See, Laclau, *Op. Cit.*
21. G. Palma, *Op. Cit.*, pp. 140-1,
22. E. Laclau, *Op. Cit.*
23. M. Sternberg, "Dependency, Imperialism and the Relations of Production", *Latin American Perspectives*, Vol. 1, No. 1, 1974, p. 78.
24. Utsa Patnaik, "On the Mode of Production in Indian Agriculture: A Reply", *Economic and Political Weekly*, Sept. 30, 1972.

25.   Bill Warren, "Imperialism and Capitalist Industrialisation: Myths of Underdevelopment", *New Left Review*, Sept-Oct., 1973.

26.   Alec Nove, "On Reading Andre Gunder Frank", *The Journal of Development Studies*, Vol. 10, Nos. 3 and 4, April-July 1974.

27.   G. Palma *Op. Cit.*, p. 140.

28.   G. Frank, *Dependent Accumulation and Underdevelopment*, Monthly Review Press, New York, 1979.

29.   R. Brenner, "The Origins of Capitalist Development: A Critique of Neo-Smithian Marxism", *New Left Review*, No. 104, July – August, 1977, pp. 25-92.

30.   G. Palma, *Op. Cit.*, p. 141.

31.   Keith Griffin and John Gurley, "Radical Analyses of Imperialism, The Third World and the Transition to Socialism: A Survey Article", *Journal of Economic Literature*, Sept., 1985, p. 1101.

32.   Sheila Smith has given an excellent precise summary of Samir Amin's work. See, S. Smith, "The Ideas of Samir Amin: Theory or Tautology?", *Journal of Development Studies*, Oct., 1980, pp. 5-21. Our discussion here is partly based on this article.

33.   Samir Amin, *Imperialism and Unequal Development*, Harvester Press, Sussex, 1977, p. 107.

5 Samir Amin On Unequal Development

Samir Amin starts with the basic hypothesis that imperialism is compelled to spread capitalism on world scale. The crisis that occurred in world capitalism at the end of nineteenth century, mainly due to falling rate of profit and underconsumption, could be partially overcome by capitalist expansion in the peripheral countries (LDCs) of the world. Falling rate of return on capital at home compelled the capitalist world to search for new pastures in LDCs. From 1880 to World War II, monopoly capital was able to export capital. During the post-imperialism phase, after 1945, central capitalism organised itself to absorb surplus from the peripheral countries through militarism, capital export and unequal exchange. All these led to unleashing imperialistic design on the part of the central capitalism.[1] Amin defines this design as the perpetuation and expansion of capitalist relations abroad by force or without the spontaneous consent of the affected people. Amin observes that capitalism requires imperialism to counteract the adverse effects on profit maximisation. In the process of imposed extraverted accumulation, the peripheral economies find themselves distorted and disarticulated and in the midst of several modes of production. In such a case, the growth of capitalism is blocked and underdevelopment becomes a permanent feature.

Samir Amin's main thesis can be discussed with reference to his main works: *Accumulation on a World Scale* (1974), *Unequal Development* (1976) and *Imperialism and Unequal Development* (1977). My schematic presentation of his basic thesis would be based on three major themes.[2] *First*, I will discuss Amin's argument about the necessity of an analysis at the world level. *Second*, I will concentrate on his characterisation of peripheral economies. *Third*, I will elaborate Amin's characterisation of economic relationship between centre and periphery.

57

Exposition of Samir Amin's Basic Thesis

Samir Amin has studied the polarisation thesis in great detail. He has analysed world capitalism in terms of two categories, namely centre and periphery. These two concepts are related to the problem of expansion of capitalism in general.[3] These concepts are essential for those who have a vision of capitalism which is neither western-centred nor economistic. Those who reject these concepts inevitably fall into the revisionist trap. In the discussion on analysis at the world level, Amin has pointed out many differences between centre and periphery.

The basic difference between centre and periphery is that capitalist relations in the centre are developed on the basis of the expansion of the home market, whereas these relations are introduced from outside in the case of periphery. In the centre, there is tendency of the capitalist mode of production to become exclusive. But it is not exclusive in the case of periphery. Another difference between centre and periphery is that in the centre, there is distinct polarisation of social classes into bourgeoisie and proletariat. On the other hand, at the periphery, since capitalism is introduced from outside, it is not exclusive, and at the same time, there is no perfect polarisation of classes. The social structure of the periphery is a truncated structure that can only be understood with reference to the world social structure.[4] The structure in the periphery is truncated because it is dominated by the absentee metropolitan bourgeoisie. The centre, moreover, has higher labour productivity and wages. Wages and labour productivity are lower at the periphery. In the centre, capitalism is characterised by autocentric accumulation, i.e. accumulation without external expansion of the system. Such a type of capital accumulation is not possible in the periphery, since the peripheral economy exists only as an appendage of the central economy; peripheral society is, in a sense, incomplete. What is missing in such a society is the metropolitan bourgeoisie whose capital operates as the essential dominating force.

In explaining the necessity of world scale, in a macro-economic perspective, Amin has considered the distinctions between the centre and periphery. He further explains centre-periphery distinction by considering the fact that in an autocentric economy, there is an organic relation between the two terms of the social contradiction--bourgeoisie and proletariat. The autocentric economy is self-sufficient and independent, but peripheral economy is extraverted. One can now present the essential points of differences between the centre and periphery in the form of chart (see next page).

According to Amin, typologies of underdeveloped countries are superficial because such typologies concentrate on appearances which mask the underlying unity of the phenomenon of underdevelopment.[5] LDCs are a piece of a single machine which is the capitalist world economy. This is the reason why it is impossible to have a perfect analysis of any one underdeveloped country in isolation from the world capitalist system. Such an analysis would simply emphasise appearances and would be misleading. The peripheral economies are without any dynamism of their own; but the central economies have internal dynamism. Amin observes that there are various forces which will propel the world system. As a matter of fact, the theory of underdevelopment and development is a theory of accumulation of capital on a world scale. In his book, *Accumulation on a World Scale*, the dynamics of the system have been explained by a single tendency: the tendency of the rate of profit to fall remains the essential and permanent expression of the basic contradiction of the system.[6] However, later on, Amin has explained the dynamics in terms of the inherent tendency of the capitalist mode of production to raise the surplus value and the search for higher profits, without relating them to the trend in the rate of profit.[7]

I should now analyse Amin's characterisation of the nature of peripheral economy. According to Samir Amin, all peripheral or satellite countries have the following four main characteristics: (i) the predominance of agrarian capitalism, (ii) a local, mainly merchant, bourgeoisie that is dominated by foreign capital, (iii) the growth of large bureaucracy, which substitutes for the leadership of an urban bourgeoisie, and (iv) incomplete polarisation, which takes the form of masses of poor peasants, urban unemployed people and many marginal workers, who have not developed completely into a proletarian class. As a result, the peripheral countries have experienced extraverted form of development of local capitalism.

Distinction Between Central Capitalism and Peripheral Capitalism

Central Capitalism	Peripheral Capitalism
Capitalist relations develop on the basis of expansion of home market	Capitalist relations are imposed from outside

Pure capitalist mode of production exists	Pre-capitalist mode of production exists
Autocentric accumulation is present. Accumulation is voluntary	Autocentric accumulation is absent. Accumulation is extraverted or distorted
Economy has an independent and complete existence	Economy is an appendage-truncated part of the centre
There is complete society	The society is incomplete
Polarisation of classes: Bourgeoisie and Proletariat	No polarisation of classes
There are internal dynamics	There are no internal dynamics
Capitalism is exclusive	Capitalism is not exclusive
Wage level is high	Wage level is low
Development is articulated	Development is disarticulated (distorted)

These countries cannot achieve development of their own momentum, but are reduced to an incomplete and extraverted development of local capitalism.[8] Moreover, the central capitalism also imposes an unequal exchange between it and the periphery in which the periphery is exploited through trade. Amin observes that peripheral countries experience extreme unevenness of development, disarticulation of the economy and a development process that is not cumulative. The dominance of foreign capital over the periphery means distorted type of development. The periphery, in order to develop itself and eliminate distortions, incurs huge amounts of debt from the central capitalism, and in this way, the periphery ultimately finds itself in the debt trap.

The peripheral capitalist mode of production has the dual feature of a modern technology and low wages within the framework of the capitalist social organisation. The productivity cannot be very high in the peripheral countries. The labour is cheap, but its productivity is also low. The

60

peripheral countries are characterised by the pre-capitalist mode of production.

The differences existing between central capitalism and peripheral capitalism have been called *distortions* by Amin.[9] Capitalism in the peripheral is imposed from outside, and the distortions are mainly caused by the introduction of foreign capital. Peripheral capitalism is characterised by the following three kinds of distortions:

(i)   There is distortion towards export activities (extraversion).

(ii)   There is abnormal enlargement (hypertrophy) of the tertiary sector.

(iii)   There is distortion towards light branches of activity (light industries) and the use of modern production technique.

The hypertrophy of the tertiary sector reflects the difficulties of realising surplus value at the centre and limitations of peripheral development – high rate of unemployment and inadequate industrialisation. The second type of distortion (hypertrophy) is expressed in excessive rise in government expenditure and a crisis in public finance. The development policies in the periphery are different from those in the centre. According to Amin, underdevelopment is not manifested in particular levels of per capita production, but in certain special structural features. There are many such structural features of underdevelopment in peripheral countries. Some of these features are: extreme unevenness in the distribution of income and in the system of prices transmitted from the centre, disarticulation and economic domination by the centre. Amin observes that as economic growth proceeds, the features of underdevelopment are accentuated. In the peripheral countries, whatever is the rate of growth of income achieved, autocentric growth becomes impossible.

Some of the peripheral countries (Hong Kong, Taiwan and so on) which have achieved some industrial growth and are now exporting finished products are simply showing a new form of inequality. Most of the LDCs still suffer from balance of payments problems and none has been able to achieve self-sustained economic growth. In such countries, there is still the domination of the central capitalism which prevents the formation of a national bourgeoisie. Only a middle class develops with the consumption pattern and ideology of the world system.

In the peripheral countries, economic growth is blocked because such countries are dominated by the centre.[10] LDCs are prevented from accumulating capital because such capital is sent away from the peripheral countries. Since there is domination by the centre, the development of underdevelopment is neither regular nor cumulative. Development in such countries is somewhat jerky and discontinuous. All these are manifested in a *double crisis* of external payments and of public finance.[11] Such a crisis is inevitable and frequent in LDCs. With economic growth, none of the bad features of LDCs are weakened, rather these features are accentuated.[12]

Having discussed the features of peripheral economies, as above, we can now elaborate Amin's characterisation of the economic relations between centre and peripheral countries. This has been discussed in his book, *Imperialism and Unequal Development*. In this discussion, Amin has mainly concentrated on the problem of unequal exchange as discussed by Arghiri Emmanuel. Amin has not accepted many points of view of Emmanuel. Amin says that two aspects of the theory of unequal exchange can be said to be essential. The first is the pre-eminence of *world values* and the second is the universal character of capitalist commodity alienation based on the direct or indirect sale of labour power. While in a capitalist system, the rate of profit is equalised, the remuneration of labour varies from country-to-country because labour is immobile. The transformation of international values into international prices implies the transfer of value from some nations to others. Since all products are international commodities, the same quantity of labour used up in different parts of the world will also give rise to a single world value. It is clear that if the labour-hour in all countries creates the same value, while the labour power in one of the countries has a lower value (lower real wages), the rate of surplus value is necessarily higher. Amin finds that surplus value generation is generally higher in LDCs.

Amin is of the opinion that the real case of unequal exchange will be present when the rates of surplus value are different in different countries, and the transfer of value takes place not as a result of different organic compositions of capital but because of the immobility of labour. In fact, the immobility of labour is responsible for the variation in real wages in different countries.[13] Amin observes that in the periphery, the pre-eminence of world values may be overshadowed by the appearance of non-capitalist mode of production. But in reality, direct producers are dominated by capital. The pre-eminence of world values constitutes the essence of the unity of the world system. If the world system were regarded merely as a

62

juxtaposition of autonomous national system, then international trade could not be analysed objectively through the analysis of the law of value.

Samir Amin has also analysed in his own way the theory of unequal exchange. He claims that his analysis of unequal exchange is superior to that of Emmanuel. According to him, his analysis is the only analysis that permits a correct definition of unequal exchange. Amin's correct definition is: the exchange of products whose production involves wage differentials greater than those of productivity.[14] The lack of internal correspondence at the periphery between the level of development of the productive forces and the value of the labour power generates the vicious circle of peripheral development. Amin's analysis of the theory of unequal exchange enables him to reject two myths of Emmanuel's analysis of unequal exchange. The *first* myth that Amin has rejected is that development can be achieved by an artificial increase of the independent variable (*i.e.* wage). Amin also points out that it is not proper to say, as Emmanuel wrongly puts it, that multinational corporations are the agents of development.[15] Amin observes that the analysis of unequal exchange shows that international capital certainly finds it profitable at the periphery because the rate of surplus value is higher there. He also notes that the peripheral mode reproduces itself both in economic terms (distortions) and also in political terms (specific class alliances). The *second* myth exploded by Amin is that the proletariat at the centre benefits from unequal exchange. On the other hand, Amin believes that high wages at the centre are mainly due to the high level of development of productive forces (*i.e.* higher productivity), and not due to international transfers.

Amin has critically discussed Emmanuel's theory of unequal exchange. Amin has pointed out a few errors in Emmanuel's theory. *Firstly*, Emmanuel wrongly treated wages as an independent variable, autonomously determined in every economy. He has not analysed wages in terms of dialectic between the laws of accumulation and the class struggle. According to Amin, such an approach is wrong on the part of Emmanuel. *Secondly*, Emmanuel has treated exports from the periphery as specific. This implies that he has separated the analysis of exchange form the analysis of production, which is not strictly permitted.

Unequal exchange is internally accompanied by unequal internal exchange at the periphery. Amin observes that such a behaviour will reproduce the system, if low wages are maintained despite modern technology. Thus, proletarianisation must be slowed down and precapitalist mode of production must be exploited. According to Amin, the distortions of peripheral capitalism do involve a problem of surplus absorption. However, this is solved by means of transfer of surplus and capital to the centre, and also through the consumption of luxury goods in the periphery. Such a type of consumption is permitted by the import of foreign technology and culture and also by the development of protected import-substituting industries. But in any case, broadly, the dependent system is reproduced. The bourgeoisie stops being a national entity. It does not satisfy the historical function of primitive capital accumulation. It always tries to protect the precapitalist mode of production to dominate the peripheral country. It also tries to make wasteful expenditure and absorb the surplus value through the consumption of luxury goods. Amin rightly asserts that dependency is not imposed but is necessary to generate the surplus in the peripheral countries.[16]

Gulalp demonstrates that Amin's work contains three different theories that can explain underdevelopment. These theories are: primitive accumulation, international specialisation, and inequality in the wage levels between different countries. By primitive accumulation, Amin means the transfer of surplus. However, the effect of the transfer of surplus on the centre and the periphery has not been very clearly explained by Amin.[17]

According to Amin, the rise of monopolies at the end of the nineteenth century created the conditions for wages in the centre to rise together with productivity while wages in the periphery remained low. Until then, exchange was equal, i.e. products were exchanged at their values. But since then, unequal exchange started due to the discrepancy in the wage level.[18] Therefore, insofar as primitive accumulation through unequal exchange constitutes a cause of underdevelopment, it is ultimately the result of the difference in the behaviour of wages between the centre and the periphery.

Amin asserts that international specialisation started when capitalism became a world system, and this was the result of Industrial Revolution.[19] However, a peripheral situation is not related to the specialisation in the export of certain products, because the kind of products exchange has evolved, and therefore, the initial form of specialisation has significantly changed. But in spite of all these, the situation in the periphery has remained more or less the same, due to discrepancy in the wage level. The impact of specialisation on the periphery has essentially remained the same. It has led to a number of *distortions* which have blocked the road for development. Amin is of the opinion that inequality in wages, due to historical reasons, constitutes the basis of a specialisation and a system of international prices that perpetuate this inequality.[20]

Inequality in the wage level can explain both primitive accumulation as well as international specialisation. In Amin's analysis, the existence of *autocentric accumulation* characterises the central capitalism, and its absence characterises the periphery. Autocentric accumulation means accumulation without external expansion of the system. Such an accumulation is possible theoretically if real wages increase at a given calculable rate. In the periphery, the principal articulation is completely absent. According to Amin, low wages in the periphery lead to a deficiency in demand as a result of which mass consumer goods industry is not sufficiently developed. This implies a distortion in the economy and a lack of self-reliance. The reason for the low level of wages in the periphery is mainly due to the fact that capitalism is not exclusively present in the periphery.

Amin has shown a typology of underdevelopment in which he describes three factors which account for the diversity of peripheral economies.[21] These factors: (i) the structure of the precapitalist formation at the moment of its integration into the world market; (ii) the economic forms of international contact; and (iii) the political forms which accompanied the integration. These factors have led many economists to deny the unity of phenomenon of underdevelopment because these factors produce diversity of the real models of underdevelopment. Many economists consider that there are only underdeveloped economies not underdevelopment. However, according to Amin, the latter is nevertheless a fact. Amin asserts that the unity of the phenomenon of underdevelopment lies in the peripheral character that is common to all LDCs in relation to capitalism and not in the mere appearances. Amin asserts that unity of the phenomenon of underdevelopment lies in the peripheral character that is common to all LDCs in relation to capitalism and not in the mere appearances. Amin claims that the diversity among LDCs is superficial, disguising the essential unity. However, Amin's work is mainly a work on the periphery and its relations with the centre. He thinks that in LDCs, the sectors are merely juxtaposed and are not properly integrated. Thus, the analysis of national economies is meaningless because such economies cannot be properly understood except at the world level.

I am now in a position to summarise the essential points of Samir Amin's main thesis on unequal development. Amin points out that central capitalism enters into the peripheral countries and creates mainly three types of distortions. *Firstly*, it gives more attention to export activities and extra-version of the economy. The export activities dislocate the internal production structure. *Secondly*, the entry of central capitalism into the periphery changes the technique of production in such a way that light industries are encouraged and technology transfer by the central capitalism goes on rampantly. This creates some sort of technological dependence. *Thirdly*, the entry of central capitalism into the periphery also distorts the tertiary sector in such a way that it becomes disproportionately larger as compared to the other sectors of the economy. As a result, many people in this sector are absorbed with low level of productivity and income. In other words, tertiary sector becomes the abode of low productivity, low income and disguised unemployment and underemployment.

In order to eliminate these distortions, and also for launching development programmes, the LDCs incur huge debts from the centre, and they also participate in the unequal exchange with the centre. Because of these two main operations, sufficient amount of surplus is taken away from the LDCs. The surplus is transferred to DCs. The inevitable result is the underdevelopment of the periphery. And once the periphery is put to the morass of underdevelopment, it once again becomes dependent on the central capitalism, and this process continues.

But how to get out of this impasse? Amin observes that LDCs have no freedom of manoeuvre in relation to world capitalism. "...So long as the underdeveloped country continues to be integrated in the world market, it remains helpless....". The possibilities of local accumulation are nil.[22] It is true so long as the dogma of the periphery is without economic means of action in relation to the multinational corporation's monopolies.[23] Amin asserts that there is no point in developing forms of financial control. In fact, the creation of a national currency confers on the local authorities no power in reality of effective control as long as the country is included and integrated with the world market, and its position *vis-à-vis* the position of world capitalism is not challenged. LDCs are prone to have all the business fluctuations of the developed capitalist economies.

The fluctuations in the value of the currencies of DCs will ultimately affect the LDCs. In the same way, the price structure of DCs is easily transmitted to the LDCs. This assertion is true as we find in modern times that the inflation of developed countries is exported to the poor developing countries. In the context of the world economy, money becomes the outward form of an essential relation of dominance. Under these circumstances, Amin aptly says that economic policy at the national level in a peripheral capitalist economy is largely ineffective.

As economic growth in the periphery proceeds, so also develops underdevelopment. Amin opines that autonomous and self-sustained growth is impossible in LDCs irrespective of the level of per capital output. Since no development is possible, it is necessary to have a complete break with the world capitalist system. This will provide the necessary condition for the genuine development. According to Amin, development is hampered by the outflow of surplus from the periphery. If some steps are taken, economic growth may occur but not economic development because development is structural in nature, which cannot be so easily changed. Development is possible when the tie with the central capitalism is snapped. Some sort of delinking is required from the centre for the development of productive forces. Amin observes that socialism is necessary because it is a means to achieve autocentric accumulation. According to him, socialism is a better alternative than compradorised or peripheral capitalism.[24]

Critical Appraisal

Samir Amin's analysis is full of useful information and ideas about the nature of peripheral economy and the causes of its underdevelopment. However, his analysis is not free from blemishes. *First*, Charles Barone reproves Amin for his excessive eclecticism. Barone says that Amin's thesis that capitalism has undergone profound transformations over the years changing the essential character of capitalism is not true. Moreover, his analysis of capitalism is based on exchange relations and not on production relations.

Second, Barone has pointed out that Amin's dependency analysis is superficial surface analysis. He fails to properly analyse the mode of production in LDCs. To Barone, Amin is an inconsistent Marxist.

Third, Amin fails to integrate his analysis with the transformation of class structures and the changing nature of capital accumulation process.

Fourth, the distortions which Amin takes to characterise periphery cannot be considered to be valid for the whole history of the periphery. Any change in the form of peripheral economy would imply that his description of the distortions collapses.[25]

Fifth, Amin has a unitary vision of development of an "all" or "nothing" type of polarity. To him, development is a purely and only a centre-determined process. This unitary vision is ahistorical and fails to take account of the historical specificities of the Third World experience. [26]

Sixth, there is a contradiction in Amin's analysis. Berstein observes that the concept of *autocentric accumulation* necessarily rules out the concept of world system, but Amin had both these concepts in his theory.[27] Capital accumulation in the cores, as is well-known, depends on the peripheral exploitation. In such a context, it does not sound very logical to speak about autocentric accumulation. Metropolitan capitalism in Amin's theory requires periphery.

Seventh, if the basis of unequal exchange is the wage differentials, then there can be unequal exchanges between many DCs because there are wage differential between them. It is not clear how it can be an exclusive characteristic of trade between the centre and periphery alone.[28]

Eighth, there seems to be a contradiction in Amin's analysis of unequal exchange.[29] Theoretically, for unequal exchange to be valid, wage differentials must be greater than productivity differentials. Amin says that high wages in the centre are due to mainly high level of development of productivity forces (productivity). Thus, productivity of the centre may be several times greater than the productivity in the periphery. If it is true, then it contradicts the basis of unequal exchange.

Ninth, Amin says that national economies do not have the power to manoeuvre and that their economic policies are ineffective. These observations are not really correct. Manoeuvrability depends on the degree and the nature of the domestic state. A highly progressive state can very well formulate and implement economic policies. This is true of many LDCs of our times.

Tenth, Amin's suggestion of decentralisation and nationalisation of capital is against the laws of development of human society and is utopian.[30]

Eleventh, as Amin wrongly suggests, breaking away with the central capitalism may have dangerous consequences, as in the case of Kampuchea. It is neither possible nor desirable for all types of LDCs. Amin has called LDCs as capitalists, although merchant/commercial capitalism pre-dominates there, and precapitalist structures are not destroyed but simply reinforced.

Lastly, Gulalp has observed that Amin has not made clear the mechanism and significance of primitive accumulation process. [31]

However, in spite of the above points of criticism, Amin's analytical umbrella seems to be much wider and it includes the analysis of the impacts of imperialism, unequal exchange and central capitalism on the underdevelopment of LDCs. His basic objective of preparing a developmentalist critique of capitalism and evaluating capitalism with reference to the development of productive forces has been fulfilled. Amin has never concentrated exclusively on the problem of dependency *per se*. Amin's analysis of unequal development is more or less than a mere dependency analysis.

Notes

1.   Samir Amin, *Unequal Development*, Harvester Press Sussex, 1976, p. 294.
2.   Samir Amin, *Accumulation on a World Scale*, Harvester Press, Sussex, 1974, pp. 166-68.
3.   Ibid., p. 123.
4.   Samir Amin, *Imperialism and Unequal Development*, Op. Cit., p. 277.
5.   K. Griffin and John Gurley, *Op. Cit*, pp. 1104-05.
6.   Samir Amin, *Unequal Development*, Op. Cit., Ch. 4.
7.   Ibid. p. 288.
8.   Ibid. p. 289
9.   Ibid. p. 292.
10.   Samir Amin, *Imperialism and Unequal Development*, Op. Cit., p. 188.
11.   Ibid, p. 211.
12.   Samir Amir, *Imperialism and Unequal Development*, Op. Cit., p. 222. Amin believes that such a view will take us back to Rostow's analysis.
13.   Ibid, p. 211.
14.   H. Gulalp, "Debate on Capitalism and Development: The Theories of Samir Amin and Bill Warren",Capital and Class, *Spring, 1986*, p. 141.
15.   Samir Amin, *Unequal Development*, Op. Cit., pp. 187-88.
16.   Ibid., pp. 157 and 183.
17.   Ibid., p. 151.
18.   Samir Amin, *Accumulation on a World Scale*, Op. Cit., pp. 166-67.
19.   Ibid, p. 131.
20.   Ibid, p. 392, and *Unequal Development*, Op. Cit., p. 201.
21.   Samir Amin, "Expansion or Crisis of Capitalism?", *Third World Quarterly*, April 1983.
22.   H. Gulalp, *Op. Cit.*, p. 156.
23.   H. Gulalp, Ibid, p. 155.
24.   H. Bernstein, "Sociology of Underdevelopment versus Sociology of Development", in D. Lehmann (ed.), *Development Theory: Four Critical Studies*, Frank Cass, 1979, pp. 91-92.
25.   S. Smith, *Op. Cit.*, p. 16.
26.   Loc. Cit.

27. Rohini Hensman, "Capitalist Development and Underdevelopment: Towards a Marxist Critique of Samir Amin", *Economic and Political Weekly*, April, 17, p. 607.

28. H. Gulalp, *Op. Cit.*, p. 141.

29. Keith Griffin and John Gurley, "Radical Analyses of Imperialism. The Third World and the Transition to Socialism: A Survey Article", *Journal of Economic Literature*, Sept, 1985, p. 1110.

30. *Loc. Cit.*

31. Subrata Ghatak, *Monetary Economics in Developing Countries*, Macmillan, London, 1981, p. 71.

6 The Structuralist Models

Structuralist model of development and underdevelopment considers the less developed countries as being beset with institutional and structural economic rigidities, and caught up in a dependence-dominance relationship with the developed countries. However, it should be noted that there is not one structuralist model, but there are at least two models of structuralism. Structuralist models present a variety of different approaches which develop in different ways the idea that certain structural characteristics of LDCs can be said to be responsible for their economic backwardness. The economic backwardness may be due to the direct consequence of structural causes or may be caused by the structural distortions as a result of harmful international relations. In the present analysis, I will consider only two types of structuralist models for explaining economic underdevelopment of a group of countries of the world.

Generalised Structuralist Model (GSM)

An early theory which does not meet all the requirements of a dependency theory of development and whose authors do not meet all the requirements of radical writers is known as the theory of *structuralism.*[1] This theory has been popularised by a number of writers like Raul Prebisch, Hans Singer, Gunnar Myrdal, Dudley Seers, Hollis Chenery, Celso Furtado, Joseph Grunwald and David Felix. All these writers, however, do not have exactly the same opinion about every aspect of structuralism . Their ideas vary in minor details; but they have broadly the same schematic thinking about structuralism. The ideas which are common among these writers can be discussed under a *generalised structuralist model.* The school of thought emerged largely and appropriately in Latin America where political independence was achieved rather early.[2] The generalised structuralist model (GSM) was concerned with the explanation for the underdevelopment of peripheral countries, particularly South America. GSM was concerned with incomplete, unsteady and inflationary problems of these countries. The GSM tried to explain away the problems with reference to the rigidities and inelasticities of economic structure of these countries. The model found a good explanation in the situation of limited possibility in the production of food grains in these countries. The model pointed out that in spite of increased demand for food grains, the production cannot be increased because of supply rigidities and certain inappropriate institutional arrangements of these initial conditions not only for inflation but also for the backwardness of these regions. Given the initial conditions of rigidities and inelasticities, there can be a good number of propagating mechanisms which give rise to many types of distortions and underdevelopment.

The economies of these countries are characterised by mainly four important factors. *Firstly*, these countries, as pointed out earlier, are characterised by rigidities and inelasticities in the matter of supply of agricultural commodities. *Secondly*, the government expenditure in such countries is much higher than a governmental income, and the rate of growth of government expenditure is much higher than the rate of growth of the economy itself. *Thirdly*, these countries are inflation-ridden. *Lastly,* the magnitude of import is much greater than that of exports, and as a result, there is deficit in the current account of the balance of payments. In such a situation, the government depreciates domestic currency. But unfortunately, it cannot solve the problem of balance of payments but instead it creates more inflation in the process.

How does the GSM work? To start with, the GSM approach points out that there is a tendency for food supply to lag behind the demand generated by the expansion of income in the non-agricultural sector, which is concomitant of economic development and that this causes food prices to rise.[3] It should be noted that the supply of food cannot be increased owing to rigidities and inelasticities. GSM postulates that the agricultural production responds very sluggishly to price and other stimuli partly owing to defective patterns of land tenure system. These patterns are survivors of precapitalists relations of production in which bonded labour, absentee management, autocratic labour relations and monopoly power disturbed sensitive responses to economic and social *status quo*.[4] Because of all these reasons, economic growth was accompanied by increases in food prices. An increase in food prices will ultimately increase the money wages. This will force the monetary authority to increase the stock of money, and this will result in inflationary spiral.

There is also foreign exchange constraint in the developing countries. This makes it impossible to import sufficient food to prevent a rise in its relative price. As noted earlier, an increase in wages as a result of increase in food prices, will lead to further increase in demand and a further rise in food prices. These countries experience growth of imports that often exceeds the growth of exports. Exports consist of primary products and imports consist of manufactured articles. The foreign exchange constraint is the cause of the introduction of industrialisation policies based on import substitution. Such policies ultimately tend to raise the prices of industrial goods and also incomes in the industrial sector. It should be borne in mind that these policies are associated with protective measures which find expression in inflation.

The primary products which are exported from LDCs fetch lower prices but the articles which are imported are more costly. The terms of trade are against the LDCs and in favour of DCs. Therefore, many LDCs are compelled to practise import substitution which raises domestic prices and often creates an inflationary spiral. It is extremely important to realise that GSM approach does not deny that an inflationary process will require an expansion of the money supply. In case money supply is not increased, the situation will lead to either a rise in unemployment or a fall in output in the industrial sector when wages rise as a result of a rise in food prices. A fall in output is bound to aggravate social tension which may create class struggle and warfare. Structuralists will argue that it is preferable to allow money supply to rise in such a situation. The GSM approach observes that monetary growth is in large part endogenous and a more fundamental underlying cause of inflation. However, the GSM approach believes that monetary policies will not be able to correct these structural weaknesses, and hence, could not be employed successfully in peripheral countries.

Another very important structural characteristic of LDCs relates to the nature of their tax system and budgetary processes which are particularly prone to perpetuate inflation, once it is started. The tax system in these countries is characterised by low inflation elasticities in the sense that when the general price level goes up, the real value of taxes goes down. This is so because many taxes are fixed in money terms, or only adjusted to inflation very slowly. Moreover, there are also various types of collection lags in LDCs, so that by the time taxes are collected, their value in real terms goes down. In other words, in the matter of taxation, the government is a loser.

But the expenditure side of the budget shows a completely different picture. In such a case, there is evidence that government expenditures tend to be fixed in real terms. Thus, when prices rise, the money value of expenditure also goes up proportionately. The crucial consequence of these two budgetary features is that when inflation begins to rise for whatever initial reason, the fiscal deficit tends to widen, because whereas the income of the government (tax being a major source of income) goes down, the expenditure goes up (because expenditure is fixed in real terms). As the deficit of the government goes on increasing as a result of inflation, it has to be financed by means of borrowing from the Central Bank. This will lead to monetary expansion and consequent increase in prices. It should be noted that capital markets in LDCs are unable to finance the growing volume of government deficit. This is another structural feature of a developing country.[5]

The initial price rise which sets this process in motion can be caused by a number of circumstances. The GSM approach has given emphasis on the following important causes: [6]

Firstly, a rise in the demand for food as a consequence of an increase in the non-agricultural income may initially set in motion the inflationary process.

Secondly, a fall in the supply of food and other agricultural products following a bad harvest may also start the inflationary process. Even when the price level goes up, food supply cannot be increased in LDCs, owing to many structural constraints.

Thirdly, a fall in export earnings with a resulting fall in imports due to a foreign exchange constraint, may reduce domestic availability of importable goods. The fall in export earnings may be a temporary phenomenon, or may reflect more deep-rooted characteristics of the demand for exports.

In all the above cases, there is a close relation between money and prices. The GSM approach shows that inflation can be mainly started by increased money supply which may be caused by two main factors, namely, wage increase and an increase in real budget deficit. Wage increase occurs primarily due to the structural rigidities and inelasticities of the agricultural sector to increase food production, and hence, causes an increase in food prices. Similarly, inflation resulting from structural factors, is mainly responsible for the widening of real budget deficit. But wage increase and an increase in budget deficit lead to further inflation which again in turn leads to wage increase and an increase in real budget deficit. The generalised structuralist model has two important feedback effects in the form of an impact on money growth from an inflation-induced rise in the real budget deficit, and a feedback from the realised inflation rate to the budget deficit and the wage determination process. The generalised structuralist model does not explicitly consider the problem of dependency in relation to economic backwardness. The association between external relations and internal structure has been clearly brought out by the model presented by Dos Santos. In the following section, I, therefore, discuss Santos's model.

Dos Santos's Structuralist Model of Dependence (DSM)

A more genuine theory of dependency has been supplied by Dos Santos. According to him, dependency arises because "...some countries can expand through self-impulsion, while others, being in a dependent position, can only expand as a reflection of the dominant countries, which may have positive or negative effects on their immediate development...".[7] This theory explains underdevelopment in terms of the manner in which the colonies had been integrated into the world economy by the advanced capitalist countries. The dependent countries had turned into suppliers of primary commodities and importers of manufactured goods. The structure of production and consumption became dislocated as a result. The LDCs were producing goods they never used and using goods they never produced. Their progress depends on their ability to balance through trade. Purchase depends on sale. If the LDCs could not sell their products in sufficient quantity, they would be unable to buy from the DCs machinery and equipment to create new industries and jobs. In this way, the problems of underdevelopment were redefined in terms of trade relations with the DCs who were enjoined to offer favourable concessions.[8]

According to Dos Santos, underdevelopment, far from constituting a state of backwardness prior to capitalism, is rather a consequence and a particular form of capitalist development, known as dependent capitalism.[9] Dependency, as Santos puts it, is a conditioning situation in which the economies of one group of countries are conditioned by the development and expansion of others.[10] A relationship of interdependence between two or more economies or between such economies and the world trading system becomes a dependent relationship. The basic situation of dependency causes these countries to be both backward and exploited. DCs can extract surplus from the dependent countries. Santos observes that dependency is based on international division of labour which allows industrial development to take place in some countries, while restricting it in others, whose growth is conditioned by and subjected to the power centres of the world.[11]

In Santos's schema, there are two structures – external and internal. Both the structures are contradictory, but the movement is produced through the dynamics of the contradictions between the two. And Santos observes that there is the priority of external over the internal structure.[12] Underdevelopment is produced by the action of the external sector over the internal sector. The concept of dependence considers the internal situation of LDCs as part of the world economy, and it is a part of the process of the world expansion of capitalism. When capitalism of the DCs is integrated with the LDCs, the underdevelopment becomes a consequence and a part of the process. In such a process, the relations produced become unequal and combined. The relation is unequal because the development of one part of the system occurs at the cost of the other part. The trade relations which develop in the process are monopolistic in character which ultimately draws away resources from the LDCs, and these resources are accumulated in the DCs. Similarly, the loans aids which are given to the LDCs are ultimately designed to draw away surplus from the LDCs. Moreover, the DCs try to have full control over the economies of these backward countries. A large part of the surplus generated in the poor countries is transferred to the DCs in the forms of profit and interest. Thus, LDCs lose substantial amount of their surplus and become poorer. The developed capitalist countries in many ways limit the capacity of development of LDCs through various types of methods which perpetuate underdevelopment by generating inequalities and transfer of surplus.[13]

The historic forms of dependence are conditioned by many factors. The laws of development of capitalism which are applicable in DCs become also applicable in those LDCs where capitalistic linkage has been established. Santos speaks of mainly three types of relations of dependency, namely, colonial type, industrial-financial type and industrial-technological type, and distinguishes different kinds of internal structures generated by them.[14] Dos Santos emphasises the differences and discontinuities between the different types of dependency and between the internal structures which result from them.[15] The technological – industrial dependence is perpetuated by the multi-national corporations. Every type of dependency relation corresponds to a situation which conditions not only the international relations of these poor countries but also their internal structures.

In the field of export, the production is geared in such a way that only the traditional export items are produced. These export items are mainly raw materials and agricultural products. The production of these items is determined by the demand from the hegemonic centres. The internal productive structure is characterised by rigid specialisation and monoculture in the whole region of the dependent country. However, the export sector draws population from other sectors of the economy. But the additional income from the export sector is consumed away by the owners and more prosperous employers. Moreover, labour is subjected to super-exploitation, and their consumption becomes limited. A great part of the accumulated surplus is sent away from the country by those foreigners who control the export sector. Dos Santos is of the opinion that the theory of comparative cost popularised by the bourgeois capitalist thinkers can only justify the inequalities of the world economic system and can conceal the relations of exploitation on which such a theory is based.[16]

Another form of dependency (technological dependency) is perpetrated by multinational corporations. Every developing country needs some foreign currencies for the purchase of machinery and finished goods. But the developing countries do not have sufficient foreign exchange reserves. Moreover, because of the patent rights, the foreign monopolistic firms prefer to transfer their machines in the form of capital rather than as commodities for sale. The multinational firms also try to help the LDCs by transferring technology. However, a large amount of surplus is taken away from the LDCs in the name of profit, royalty and interest. This also is accompanied by foreign political dependence and interest. Foreign capital does not really help the dependent countries. Such capital takes more money away than it contributes. This is the reason why many countries have imposed control over the foreign firms.

Another problem associated with the dependent type of industrial development is that it is strongly conditioned by the balance of payments situation. More often than not, most of dependent LDCs suffer from chronic balance of payments problems. Santos has put forward mainly three reasons for the balance of payments deficit in these countries. *Firstly,* while the price of exportable commodities is higher in the DCs, the price of importable commodities is kept much lower. Moreover, many DCs have introduced synthetic commodities which have replaced the traditional items of exports of LDCs. Secondly, foreign capital has very effective control over most of the dynamic sectors of LDCs and repatriates a large volume of profit from out of LDCs. As a consequence, the capital accounts of LDCs become highly unfavourable to dependent countries. Santos have given evidence to show that the amount of capital entering a developing country is much less than the amount of capital leaving the country. This produces an enslaving deficit in capital accounts. Moreover, many charges such as freight transport, technical fees are exorbitantly high as these are imposed by the foreign firms. Foreign capital and aid fill up the holes that they themselves have created. The real value of aid is very doubtful in the case of less developed countries. Santos has shown that it is nearly 40 per cent of the gross aid. Moreover, the aid is paid sometimes in local currencies and it is tied. The LDCs have to pay for all the aids they receive. *Thirdly,* the technology that is transferred to less developed countries is not suitable for these countries and it is applied in the low-priority sector. The technology is mostly available in the form of patents. For transferring these patents rights, the multinational firms demand either royalty payment or they convert these goods into capital and introduce them in the form of their own surplus. The technology which is supplied is very often the old and useless technology.

However, since there is lack of capital, LDCs have to borrow capital from abroad. Foreign capital is invited into LDCs and is given many facilities like exemption from the exchange control, from some types of taxation, granting of installation sites, loan facilities and so on. But the high profits obtained from such foreign capital can be reinvested freely. It has been found that a large part of the capital investment in LDCs comes from reinvestment of profit, which varies from 40 per cent to 60 per cent.[17]

Dos Santos has elaborately discussed the effects of external structure and dependency on the internal productive structure. He says that the productive system of LDCs is essentially determined by the international relations. Foreign firms extract a large amount of surplus from agriculture, mining and export sectors. The unequal and combined character of capitalist development is reproduced internally in an acute form. *Secondly,* the domestic techno-industrial structure of dependent countries responds more closely to the interest of the multinational corporations than to internal development needs.[18] *Thirdly*, the external structure and relations also produce many types of productive structure, skewed income distribution, under-utilisation of capacity and so on, which are found in advanced capitalist countries.

The accumulation of capital in such a situation is characterised by many types of dichotomies in production, distribution, wage level and so on. All this leads to a high rate of exploitation of domestic labour. A dependent type of development is also associated with unequal and combined character of international capitalist economic relations, with technological and financial control, with balance of payments deficits and also with the disturbance of the economic policies of domestic state. A dependent type of development puts limit to the growth of internal markets in LDCs. The productive structure of LDCs is affected in mainly three ways. *First,* labour force is highly exploited. *Second*, capital-intensive technology is adopted and unemployment goes up. *Third*, a large part of the surplus generated in LDCs in the form of profit is remitted out of the country. All these restrict the possible development of basic national industries in LDCs. Thus, it is clear that the alleged backwardness of LDCs is not due to a lack of integration with capitalism, but that, on the contrary, the most powerful obstacle to their full development comes from the way in which they are integrated with the international capitalist system and its laws of development.[19]

As Santos believes, underdevelopment is related to the system of world economic relation based on monopolistic control of large-scale capital and also on the control over certain economic and financial centres. The control is imposed through capital, technology and trade, all of which induce unequal and combined development in LDCs. The LDCs of today try to develop within the framework of a process of dependent production and reproduction. The system is a dependent one because it produces a productive system whose development is limited by those world relations which necessarily lead to unequal development under unequal conditions. It also divides the surplus and sends away a substantial part of it abroad.[20] Because of the dependent system, certain situations which are favourable for economic development, cannot be availed of by the LDCs; on the other hand, they reproduce underdevelopment and misery. Dependent development benefits only a limited sector and that too only temporarily.

But how to solve the problem? Santos says that a popular revolutionary government or a socialist society may be the answer. And no intermediate solution appears to be possible and successful. The dependence of LDCs cannot be overcome without a qualitative change in the internal structures and external relations.

The arguments put forward by Santos reveal that external relations influence the internal structure in such a way that trade relations, technology and finance not only distort and dislocate production but also lead to loss of surplus. All these adversely affect the balance of payments and the balanced industrial development of LDCs which become more dependent on DCs, and the same dependent relations once again are repeated. The external relation is also responsible for the loss of surplus from an underdeveloped country. The model presented by Santos believes that in the long-run, left to itself, growth will be hampered, and structural dislocation and distortions will be aggravated. The model suggests that for economic development, external dependence has to be eliminated. Unlike the GSM, Santos model is fully consistent with dependency theory. The following chart presents a comparative picture of the two models.

Distinctions Between GSM Model and DSM Model

Generalised Structuralist Model	Dos Santos Model
Internal structure is independent, autonomous and endogenous	Internal structure is not independent It is dependent on external/capitalist relation. The internal structure is exogenous
Only internal structural factors like rigidity and inelasticity are responsible for underdevelopment	External structure brings about dislocation and distortions in production, and causes loss of surplus. Those two factors are responsible for underdevelopment
In the long-run, structural defects can be cured	In the long-run, left to itself, growth will be hampered, and structural dislocation and distortions will be aggravated
For economic development, internal structure is to be changed	For economic development, external dependence has to be eliminated
Dependency theory is not fully applicable in the case of GSM	Dependency theory is fully applicable in the case of Santos model

Critical Appraisal

The structuralist models have been subjected to a number of criticisms. The problem of underdevelopment has been conceived in an essentially quantitative fashion in the structuralist model. According to Kay, this has prevented any effective criticism of the relations of production that lay at the heart of the problem. The theory lacked a revolutionary political dimension.[21] *Second*, the approach could not demolish the neo-classical basis of development theory directly. The radical structuralists were forced to import their political positions in exactly the same way as neo-classicism. They were not able to go beyond revolutionary phraseology.[22]

Third, Dos Santos's analysis of dependence is based on the experience of Latin America only, particularly Chile, and not even all the Latin American countries. His findings cannot be perhaps made applicable to other developing countries. *Fourth*, the empirical data are much against the postulates of the models of structuralism. It has been found that it is possible to have agricultural growth under certain circumstances and monetary policy in LDCs can be made effective.

Fifth, it should be noted that all rigidities are not natural in any economy. Some of the rigidities are owing to government interferences in the market process. Such interferences may lead to many types of market failures. *Sixth*, the land tenure system is not such that it cannot be changed or it has not been changed. In fact, land tenure system has been misinterpreted by the structuralist models.[23] *Seventh*, inflation in most of the LDCs is created not because of the structural factors, but because of excess money supply. The structuralist writers very often believe that inflation is mainly caused by structural factors. This is, however, not true. Monetarists argue that structural problems are a consequence of inflation rather than its cause. However, many structuralists do believe that excess money supply may be the cause of inflation in LDCs, but that excess money supply may be basically caused by structural forces. *Lastly*, the structuralist model can be said to be myopic in the sense that it does not recognise the beneficial effects of capitalist development through aid, trade and so on. Capitalist process does sometime lead to some salutary effects on the growing economy of a new country.

Notes

1.   K. Griffin and John Gurley, *Op. Cit.*, p. 1110.
2.   D. Dutton, "A Model of Self-Generating Inflation: The Argentine Case", *Journal of Money, Credit and Banking*, 1971, 3(2), pp. 245-62, and B. B. Aghevli and M. S. Khan, "Inflationary Finance and the Dynamics of Inflation: Indonesia (1951-72)", *American Economic Review*, 1970, 67 (3), pp. 390-403.
3.   Sourata Ghatak, *Op. Cit.*, p. 73.
4.   Dos Santos, "The Structure of Dependence", *American Economic Review*, May 1970, pp. 289-90. This is a representative article depicting Santos's stand on structuralism. Hence, our subsequent discussion on Santos model heavily draws on this article.
5.   Geoffrey Kay, *Development and Underdevelopment: A Marxist Analysis*, Macmillan, London, 1975, pp. 9-10.
6.   Dos Santos, "The Crisis of Development Theory and the Problem of Dependence in Latin America", Siglo, XXI, 1969. Also see, Benjamin J. Cohen, *The Question of Imperialism: The Political Economy of Dominance and Dependence*, Basic Books, New York, 1973.
7.   *Loc. Cit.*
8.   *Loc. Cit.*
9.   G. Palma, "Dependency: A Formal Theory of Underdevelopment or a Methodology for the Analysis of Concrete Situations of Underdevelopment?", World Development, Vol. 6, as given in G.M. Meier, *Leading Issues in Economic Development*, Oxford University Press, 1984, p. 142.
10.   D. Santos, "The Structure of Dependence", *American Economic Review*, May 1970, as given in C. K. Wilber (ed.), *Political Economy of Development and Underdevelopment*, Random House, USA, 1973, p. 110.
11.   G. Palma, *Op. Cit.*, p. 141.
12.   *Loc. Cit.*
13.   D. Santos, *Op. Cit.*, p. 116.
14.   D. Santos, *Op. Cit.*, p. 114. In recent years, the trend is more marked which shows that re-investment of profit is on the rise in Latin America.
15.   Dos Santos, *Op. Cit.*, p. 115.
16.   Dos Santos, *Op. Cit.*, p. 116.
17.   I. V. Levin, The Export Economies, Harvard University Press, 1964. Levin has given many examples of utilisation of surplus in DCs.
18.   G. Kay, *Op. Cit.*, p. 10.
19.   *Loc. Cit.*
20.   K. Griffin and J. Gurley, *Op. Cit.*, p. 1110.
21.   See, G. Palma, *Op. Cit.*, p. 142.
22.   Celso Furtado, *Development and Underdevelopment*, University of California Press, California, 1964, p. 129.
23.   Ibid., p. 130.

7 The Theories of Unequal Exchange

Third World Countries have been integrated with the world capitalist system which has created a division of labour on world scale, according to which, the less developed countries (LDCs) produce the primary commodities and the DCs produce manufactured goods. The income elasticity of demand for primary goods being very low, the net barter terms of trade of the primary producing countries declines over time. This is one of the ways in which the surplus from the LDCs is taken away by the DCs. The position cannot be improved by the LDCs because of the specificity in natural resources endowments and limited technological horizon. The deterioration in the terms of trade is a serious obstacle to economic development of LDCs. Two serious works in this direction were done first by Raul Prebisch (1959) and Hans Singer (1950). Their work which generally goes by the name of Prebisch-Singer thesis has been elaborated in this chapter.

The emphasis then shifted to the analysis of the distribution of gains from trade, and the relevant concept is the double factoral terms of trade (DFTT). It has been argued that DFTT has gone against the LDCs and the gains of trade have gone in favour of DCs. This has led to the widening of inequality between LDCs and DCs. In 1972, Arghiri Emmanuel put forward his thesis on unequal exchange which claims that because of differentials in wage, and through the low wages of LDCs, the DCs are able to extract a large amount of surplus value from the LDCs, and this hampers the growth process of these poor countries. In what follows, I will analyse at some length the Prebisch-Singer thesis and Emmanuel's thesis on unequal exchange.

Prebisch-Singer Thesis

The thesis propounded by Raul Prebisch and H. Singer states that in the long-run, the terms of trade move against the primary producing countries.

The thesis has prognosticated a secular deterioration of the terms of trade between the centre and the periphery. This is the principal factor retarding the growth of LDCs. According to them, the terms of trade had shifted in favour of DCs. Prebisch generalised that a long-term decline in the terms of trade of LDCs is an essential consequence of growth and trade between the centre and periphery.[1] H. Singer in 1950 propounded his thesis that opening of LDCs to trade and investment has tended to inhibit their growth.[2] Raul Prebisch's thesis came in 1950 and then 1959. The views of Prebisch and Singer are almost similar: their major conclusions and findings are the same. This is the reason why the thesis is proposed in joint names of Prebisch and Singer. Prebisch-Singer thesis is based on the following assumptions:[3]

Assumptions

Firstly, there is the functioning of a global Engel's law which states that as growth proceeds, the relative demand composition shifts away from the primary products to manufacture.

Secondly, manufacturing industries are not typically competitive, so increases in productivity are not passed on to consumers through lower prices, but are retained by the producing countries as higher profit.

Thirdly, new synthetic substitutes for primary products are bound to appear periodically, thereby diminishing the share of primary goods in the international market.

Fourthly, in LDCs, there is no strong labour organisation. Hence, wage level remains low, and terms of trade decline.

Fifthly, export market in DCs works under monopolistic conditions, but in LDCs, it is a competitive market.[4]

Sixthly, demand for the products of the periphery is rising very slowly.

Lastly, income terms of trade or capacity to import is the determining factor for economic development in LDCs.

Prebisch and Singer have argued that LDCs have sustained losses in the international trade over an extended period and the gains from the trade are mainly reaped by the developed countries. The prices of the exports of the LDCs have declined over the years, whereas the prices of their imports have risen secularly. A UN report showed that the ratio of index of prices of primary goods to that of manufactured goods showed a secular tendency to decline from 147 for the period 1876-80 to 100 in 1938.

Prebisch, Singer and Myrdal pointed out that international trade has mainly benefited the DCs and has gone against the interest of the LDCs. This secular deterioration of the terms of trade is mainly hindering the growth process of the LDCs. The DCs have the monopolistic control over the product and factor prices. This has led to the transfer of gains in the form of technological progress through rising factor incomes of developed countries; but for LDCs, the gains in productivity have been more than neutralised by the price reduction. According to Prebisch, the LDCs were unable to share the gains of technological progress derived by the DCs, but on the contrary, those poor countries could not retain their own productivity gains because of demographic pressure and technological backwardness.[5]

Prebisch's observation of the deteriorating terms of trade of LDCs was based on a study of Britain's terms of trade between 1976 – 80 and 1938 in comparison with the terms of trade of Latin American countries. During this period, there was a secular decline in the prices of raw materials in relation to the prices of manufactured goods. In DCs, factor income increased relatively more than productivity, whereas in LDCs, the increase in factor income was much less than the increase in productivity. In other words, the DCs keep the whole benefits of the technological progress of their industries; the LDCs cannot enjoy the entire cake of technological progress. The whole benefit of the technical progress in DCs which have imperfect competition is absorbed by the capitalist and the workers in the forms of higher profits and wages.

The LDCs have the worst of both the worlds. *Firstly*, productivity gains of the DCs do not percolate to LDCs. *Secondly*, when technical progress leads to productivity gains in LDCs, their product prices fall. Unlike DCs, the LDCs operate under competitive conditions. They purchase from the most expensive market and sell in the cheapest market. On the other hand, the DCs have the best of both worlds.

Another factor responsible for secular deterioration of the terms of trade against the LDCs is the long-term disparity in the demand for primary products and that for manufactured goods. Generally, income elasticity of demand for primary goods is less than unity, but that of manufactured goods is more than unity. Prebisch found that for every additional 1 per cent increase in income in USA, the demand for primary products from LDCs increased by only 0.66 per cent, whereas every additional 1 per cent increase in income in Latin America (LDCs), led to 1.5 per cent increase in import of manufactured goods from the DCs. This observation is based on Engel's law: proportion of income spent on food declines with rising income, and the proportion of income spent on luxury items increases with increasing income. Technical progress, according to Prebisch, gives rise to demonstration effect which creates new demand and wants for the new products of the DCs. Thus, import in LDCs goes on increasing.

Distinctions Between Centre and Periphery

Centre	Periphery
Trade unions very strong	Trade unions weak
Wages high	Wages low
Demand for its products increases rapidly	Demand for its products grows slowly
Export market monopolistic	Export market competitive
Exports manufactured articles and imports food and raw materials	Exports food and raw materials, and imports manufactured articles
Income elasticity of demand for import is low (less than one)	Income elasticity of demand for import is high (more than one)
Productivity gain leads to wage increase	Productivity gain does not lead to wage increase
Export prices are generally high	Export prices are generally low
Increase in factor income is more than the increase in productivity	Increase in factor income is less than the increase in productivity
Terms of trade generally improve over time	Terms of trade generally deteriorate over time

It is now possible to summarise the main points of distinction between the centre and the periphery, after Prebisch (see the following chart). The centre has strong trade unions and wages in DCs are higher than the wages in LDCs. The LDCs do not have strong trade unions. The demand for the product of the centre rapidly increases, whereas the demand for the product of LDCs only slowly goes up. Moreover, the centre mainly exports manufactured articles and imports food products and raw materials. On the other hand, LDCs export mainly food products and raw materials but import manufactured goods. There is another very basic difference between

86

the centre and the periphery. In the centre, the income elasticity of demand for import is less than one, but the income elasticity of demand for import in the case of LDCs is very high (more than one). When productivity rises in DCs, wages also rise, but this is not the case in LDCs where productivity growth does not lead to increase in wages. In the centre, export prices are generally very high, but in the periphery, the export prices are generally low. It has been found that terms of trade over the years become favourable for DCs, but they become unfavourable for LDCs. Export market is monopolistic in DCs, but it is competitive in LDCs.

Singer has pointed out that foreign investment has led to economic imperialism in LDCs.[6] According to him, foreign enclave is not interested in the development of LDCs. Foreign investment has produced three harmful consequences in LDCs. *Firstly*, foreign investment has produced many advantages for the DCs. These advantages have given cumulative multiplier effects out of the heavy profit that has been remitted from LDCs to DCs. *Secondly*, foreign investment has distorted the production pattern of LDCs in such a way that LDCs do not have sufficient scope for getting the benefits of internal and external economies and technical progress. *Thirdly*, foreign investment has also led to the worsening of the terms of trade of LDCs.

Figure 7.1 Price of Products

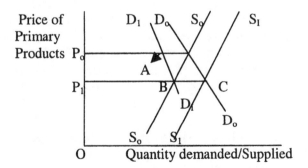

Two important facts are to be noted in this connection. *First*, whenever the productivity in LDCs grows, the prices of their products in the international market also go down. *Second*, whenever the demand for the products of LDCs goes down in the foreign market, the price level of their products also goes down. Thus, the LDCs become worse off in both the situations.

But the developed countries have the beneficial cumulative effects in both the situations as consumers of imported food and raw materials at low prices, and as producers of high-priced exportable manufactured articles. This situation can be explained with the diagram on the previous page which shows that as the demand for the products of LDCs goes down, the price level of their products comes down from P_0 to P_1. Similarly, when the supply of the primary products increases as a result of good monsoon or otherwise, the price level again comes down from P_0 to P_1.

These two factors will point out that there would be the immiserisation of growth in less developed countries, as a result of the increase in their productivity.[7] Singer noted that the popular belief that in the post-war period there has been some improvement in the terms of trade of LDCs, is not really borne out by facts. In reality, the LDCs have failed to benefit from a little rise in the prices of their products, because the extra profit is generally invested by these countries in the expansion of their production rather than in capital formation. When the prices are low, these countries cannot have the means to industrialise; similarly, when the prices are high, they are also not in a position to industrialise. Thus, LDCs fall in between two difficult situations which prevent them to from industrialising.

Hans Singer observes that since the seventies, the trend of prices has been working heavily against the sellers of food and raw materials (LDCs) and in favour of the sellers of manufactured articles (DCs). LDCs specialise in the export of food and raw materials to the developed countries. International trade for LDCs has given lesser scope for technical progress and internal and external economies and diversification. Technical progress in manufacturing countries led to a rise in income, but in primary producing countries, it led to a fall in the prices of exportable items. The LDCs use the profits for expanding their production rather than investing them on capital goods. According to him, the deterioration in the terms of trade of the LDCs is a sort of backwash effect which is a serious drag on economic development.

The arguments of Prebisch and Singer are quite similar. As a policy prescription, Prebisch is of the view that economic backwardness of LDCs cannot be overcome without industrialisation. It is also necessary for them to introduce protection. Protection does not imply restriction of imports but simply a change in their composition. Singer, however, prescribes the appropriate and optimum utilisation of foreign capital.

Critical Appraisal

First, deterioration in the net barter terms of trade does not necessarily make a country worse off, if it occurs as a result of a still greater improvement in productivity. If the cost falls too low as a consequence of productivity gain, a high income may be sustained. The examples are US wheat production and cocoa production by Gold Coast farmers.

Second, Colin Clark and Arthur Lewis arrive at diametrically opposite results from their study on the terms of trade. Britain's gain was not at cost of LDCs. Britain's exports include carriage and insurance charges but her imports include insurance and freight. During 1870 – 1938, freight charges dramatically fell, which accounted for improvement in terms of trade partially. This fact has not been noted by Prebisch and Singer. Again 69 per cent of Britain's imports came from other DCs.

Third, the statistical comparison of the crude relative prices is unrealistic, for over time, the increase in the prices of industrial goods is mainly due to improvement in quality. The quality of primary goods over time remains more or less the same.

Fourth, the thesis is mainly based on the experience of Britain. It may not be applicable to other DCs.

Fifth, all LDCs are not the importers of manufactured goods and exporters of primary goods. Similarly, all DCs are not the importers of primary goods and exporters of manufactured goods. Thus, the classificatory schema of Prebisch-Singer thesis is wrong.

Sixth, it is not true to say that economic development is mainly hampered by the deteriorating terms of trade. Development is a function of many factors, and terms of trade would represent only one such factor. In fact, LDCs have received improved ideas, technology and knowledge from the DCs.

Lastly, Haberler observes that Prebisch-Singer thesis lacks proof and is based on reckless extrapolation and faulty explanation. He opines that longrun terms of trade would not behave in the same manner for all types of exporters of primary products and importers of industrial goods. Haberler does not accept the idea of Prebisch and Singer that the prices of manufactured goods are kept high in DCs by monopolistic behaviour of trade unions and cartels. According to Haberler, Engel's law does not apply to every kind of food, and certainly it does not apply to industrial raw materials.

Despite the aforesaid points of criticism, the Prebisch-Singer thesis is not totally invalid. Although it was not proved till 1938, it seemed to be more or less correct during the post-Second War period. The study by UNCTAD (Trade and Development Report, 1981) and IMF Survey (1982) have vindicated the Prebisch-Singer thesis. The basic point of view of this thesis remains true still today.[8]

Arghiri Emmanuel on Unequal Exchange

International trade has been given an important role to play in the dependency analysis for the explanation of development and underdevelopment of the centre and periphery. In this type of analysis, Emmanuel's contribution has become noteworthy. Emmanuel has analysed underdevelopment in terms of unequal exchange, and through this theory, he has explained surplus extraction from the less developed countries (LDCs). Emmanuel contends that LDCs are selling their commodities below value and buying the commodities from DCs at a price which is above value. Thus, there is an unequal exchange between the DCs and LDCs, and this is the mechanism through which surplus is drained out from LDCs to DCs. The main ideas of Emmanuel have been incorporated in his book. *Unequal Exchange: A Study of the Imperialism of Trade* (1972). In the following discussion, I will elaborate the basic mechanism of unequal exchange as given by A. Emmanuel.

Emmanuel's Main Thesis on Unequal Exchange

A. Emmanuel propounded a very influential thesis in 1972 to explain unequal and uneven development between the centre and the periphery. The central element in his theory is the mechanism in which international exchange ratios are determined.[9] With the help of his theory of unequal exchange, Emmanuel has been able to prove that surplus from LDCs is taken away by the DCs, and as a result, the LDCs become underdeveloped. Emmanuel's theory of unequal exchange is based on the following assumptions.

Assumptions

First, organic composition of capital is not the same as between developed countries (DCs) and less developed countries (LDCs). Generally, organic composition of capital is higher in DCs and lower in LDCs.

Second, there is free flow of trade between DCs and LDCs under competitive conditions in the market.

Third, wages are different in DCs and LDCs. Wages are lower in LDCs and higher in DCs.

Fourth, rates of profit are equalised between DCs and LDCs as in Marxist tradition.

Fifth, value and price are not equal in different countries.

Sixth, there are two goods and two countries (one developed and one underdeveloped).

Seventh, even if the labour content of both the goods is the same, their prices would differ. Prices are generally higher in DCs and lower in LDCs.

Eighth, productivity of labour between the two countries does not so much vary as the wage level.

Ninth, non-labour costs are the same in both the countries.

Tenth, capital is internationally mobile but labour is not.

Lastly, the ratio of wage to marginal productivity of labour is higher in DCs than that in LDCs.

On the basis of the above assumptions, Emmanuel explained his theory of unequal exchange. He pointed out that unit cost would be lower in LDCs than the unit cost in DCs, because wages are lower in LDCs as compared to the wages in DCs. However, this is true if lower wages are not associated with lower productivity of labour. Emmanuel assumes that the productivity of labour in LDCs is not very much lower. Labour productivity does not change as much as the wage level. Thus, the truth-value of Emmanuel's theory is not disturbed by simply assuming equal productivity of labour in both the countries. If non-labour costs are the same in both DCs and LDCs, and current labour creates the same value for a period of time, the rate of profit would be higher in LDCs where wages are lower. Unequal exchange results through the movement of capital in search of higher rate of profit elsewhere. In the course of time, through price movement, there would be equalisation of the rate of profit in DCs and LDCs. Emmanuel asserts that international exchange takes place at rates which are not equal to the labour time contained in commodities. The ratio of advanced country prices to backward country prices is greater than the ratio of the labour time in advanced country commodities to the labour time in the backward country commodities.[10] Here, these two types of countries are defined in terms of wage level. In DCs, the wage level is higher, and in LDCs, wage level is lower. The theory of unequal exchange lays down that international trade helps DCs in appropriating more labour time in exchange than they generate in production, and thus, they exchange with LDCs. Through trade, surplus is transferred from LDCs to DCs, and as a result, the LDCs remain underdeveloped.

The theory of unequal exchange, as given by Emmanuel, has two interpretations: one is narrow interpretation and the other is broad interpretation. These two interpretations are discussed in the following sections.

Narrow Interpretation of Unequal Exchange

Table 7.1 The Working of the Economy with Respect to Production Sphere

	Branch I (DCs)	Branch II (LDCs)	Macro-perspective
(C) Constant Capital	80	60	140
(V) Variable Capital	20	40	6
(S) Surplus Value	20	40	60
(O) Value (C+V+S)	120	140	260
(C/V) Organic Composition of Capital	4	1.5	2.3
(S/V) Rate of Surplus Value	100%	100%	100%
(PG) Profit Rate (%)	20% *	40%*	30%
(C+V) Cost of Production	100	100	200
(Price) = Cost (C+V) plus profit	130	130	260

* The equalised rate of profit is 30%

According to Emmanuel, there is a transfer of value from a country with a low organic composition of capital to a country with a high organic composition of capital (DCs). As a consequence of the equalisation of the rate of profit, international exchange occurs at rates which are not equal to the labour time embodied in the commodities which are exchanged internationally. Arghiri Emmanuel has used the Marxian theory of transformation to show that LDCs are compelled to sell their goods at a price below their value and purchase goods of DCs at prices above their value. Let me explain the mechanism of unequal exchange by means of a Table [11] (see Table 7.1).

One can assume a fully developed capitalist sector with two branches: Branch (I) is producing the means of production, and Branch (II) is producing the means of consumption. Marx said that the rate of profit must be same in all the branches; otherwise, capital shall flow from the low-profit to high-profit branch. We can now introduce the concept of general rate of profit (PG). The working of the economy with respect to the production sphere is given in Table 7.1 In this Table, (C) represents capital cost utilised in production, (V) is the wage bill, (S) is the surplus value, (PG) is the rate of profit, (O) is total output (value), (C/V), is the organic composition of capital, (S/V) is the rate of surplus value, (C+V) is the cost of production , and price is given by cost of production plus the rate of profit, or, (C+V+PG).

The rate of profit is calculated as
$$\left[\frac{S}{C+V} \cdot \right]$$

As the Table 7.1 shows, Branch I sells its goods at the price of 130, while its value (C+V+S=) is 120. Branch II also sells the goods at 130 price, but its value is 140. If one denotes Branch I as DCs and Branch II as LDCs, it becomes clear that the DCs sell their goods at prices above their value; and LDCs sell their goods at prices below their value. Whereas price in the market is the same for both the branches, values are different for them. Thus, the exchange of commodities between these branches is unequal. It is clear from the Table that commodities produced in Branch II having a lower organic composition of capital will sell below their values to compensate for the excessive profit that would accrue to capital here if they sell at value. [12] The DCs sell their commodities to LDCs at prices above their values and purchase commodities from LDCs at prices below their values. Thus, every transaction between LDCs and DCs involves a drain of value out of LDCs.[13] This, therefore, reduces the tempo of development in LDCs.

Broad Interpretation of Unequal Exchange

In the broad interpretation of unequal exchange, one can take into account the changes in the wage level of DCs, and can explain the effects of such changes.[14] In order to explain the meaning of unequal exchange in a broad sense, one can take the help from Table 7.2. Suppose the value of wages goes up by 50 per cent in DCs. i.e. (V) rises from 20 to 30. Thus, (S) falls from 20 to 10, other things remaining the same. These changes should be appreciated with reference to our Table 7.1 (given earlier).

Table 7.2, should be read with Table 7.1 to know the changes incorporated. Table 7.2 shows that although there is no general immediate impact on LDCs (Branch II) as a result of a change in the wage level in DCs, the general rate of surplus value goes down from 100 to 71.4 per cent and the general rate of profit also goes down from 30 per cent to 23.80 per cent. Although the value of production remains the same, the prices of production are changed in such a way that they are more favourable to DCs. The terms of trade have now moved further against LDCs. Emmanuel says that increasing living standards of the workers of DCs are partly paid by the LDCs. In Table 7.2, prices of production are shown to be different in two countries. The prices are higher in DCs and lower in LDCs. The cost of production is also higher in DCs as compared to LDCs. The higher cost of production in DCs is mainly due to higher wages. Thus, by increasing the prices in this way, DCs can improve their terms of trade and extract surplus from LDCs. The situation can be explained by a simple numerical example. Let us suppose that there are two countries: one DC and one LDC, and two goods X and Y are produced both of which require 10 units of labour for their production. The wages in the two countries being different, their cost of production would also be different. Suppose, wage of one unit of labour is $2 in the DC, and $1 in the LDC. Therefore, cost of production of X in the DC will be $20; and the cost of production Y in the LDC will be $10, even if they contain the same amount of labour. Labour, therefore, is exchanged unequally between the two countries because their wages are different.

94

Here lies the crux of the broad meaning of unequal exchange. In the case of unequal exchange of this type, the prices in the market are different and the cost of production of DCs becomes higher simply because of higher wages, and the LDCs experience unfavourable terms of trade vis-à-vis the DCs. The case which is explained in Table 7.2 is a more general case of unequal exchange where not only the prices change but also the cost of production changes as a result of changes in the wage level of mainly DCs. It shows that when the wage rate in the DCs goes up, the terms of trade of LDCs become more unfavourable. As is well-known, this situation prevails in the international-trade of our times. Hence, it can more appropriately be called a more general or broader interpretation of unequal exchange. It is in this sense that unequal exchange is generally interpreted. In this type of situation, the DCs will appropriate more labour time than they generate in production. In other words, the DCs can get the commodity from the LDCs at cheaper prices than what would have been the cost in their own countries. Thus, a surplus is transferred from DCs to LDCs in larger amount. In this process of exchange, the LDCs do not get the justified value of their products. Hence they stand losers.

Table 7.2 The Working of Unequal Exchange

	Branch I (DCs)	Branch II (LDCs)	Macro-perspective
(C) Constant Capital	80	60	140
(V) Variable Capital	30	40	70
(S) Surplus Value	10	40	50
(O) Value (C+V+S)	120	140	260
(C/V) Organic Composition of Capital	2.6	1.5	2.5
(S/V) Rate of Surplus Value	33%	100%	71.4%
Cost (C+V)	110	100	210
(PG) Profit Rate (%)	23.80%	23.80%	
(Price) = Cost (C+V) plus profit	136.18	123.80	260 (approx.)

The basic thesis of unequal exchange can now be explained with the help of the diagrams given below:

Figure 7.2   **Figure 7.3**

(A)   (B)

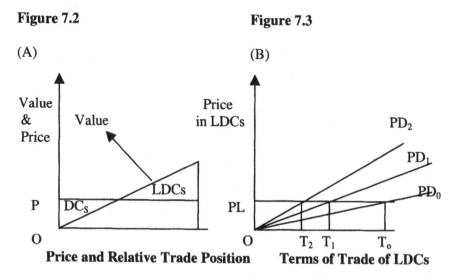

Price and Relative Trade Position   **Terms of Trade of LDCs**

In the diagram (panel A) price is taken as the same and constant for both DCs and LDCs. But DCs sell commodities at this price (OP) which is above their value, but LDCs will sell commodities at this price (OP) which is below their value. This is, then, the unequal exchange between DCs and LDCs. In fact, this is the essence of our Table 7.1.

Panel B shows that the price level of LDCs remaining unchanged at OP_L (which is below the value), the higher is the price level of DCs, the worse becomes the terms of trade (TOT) of LDCs, for there is a gradual movement of TOT towards the zero (O) as the price level of DCs goes up. Thus, when the price level of DCs is OPD_0 terms of trade position of LDCs is OT_0. However, it should be noted that this TOT position itself reflects an undesirable sub-normal position, as the price level of LDCs is less than the value of their commodities. The position of TOT in the case of LDCs gradually shrinks or worsens further when the price level of the commodities of DCs is further raised to OPD_1. When the price of DCs in OPD_2, the terms of trade (TOT) of LDCs is reduced to OT_2. The same is the conclusion of our Table 7.2 which analyses the meaning of unequal exchange in a broader or more general sense.

Having elaborated the meaning of unequal exchange in both narrow and general senses, I can now briefly summarise the basic idea of the theory of unequal exchange as given by Emmanuel. The theory says that because of higher wages of DCs, the prices of their commodities remain higher than their values. When these commodities produced by LDCs by virtue of their lower wages are exchanged, the DCs take away the surplus from the LDCs. Unequal exchange mainly accounts for the growing inequality among DCs and LDCs. When the LDCs trade their products containing more or less the same amount of labour hours with the DCs,[15] there is a loss on the part of LDCs and corresponding gain on the part of DCs. Thus, by invoking the theory of unequal exchange, Emmanuel has tried to analyse the problem of underdevelopment of LDCs through a new perspective.

Critical Appraisal

Emmanuel's thesis on unequal exchange has been subjected to a number of criticisms. Many radicals have raised many objections against his thesis both from theoretical and empirical points of view. In what follows, I will present briefly some of the important points of criticisms that have been levelled against the theory of unequal exchange.

First, Emmanuel has simply concentrated on the circulation sphere, and not production sphere.[16] Bettelheim maintains that wage differentials are mainly based on the production sphere which Emmanuel has neglected. The neglect of production sphere has reduced the force of his theory considerably. It pointed out that inequality between DCs and LDCs arises mainly from the difference in the development of productive forces. According to Bettleheim, it is misleading to characterise the trade between DCs and LDCs as a matter of exploitation of LDCs. Bettelheim contends that unequal exchange does not prevent in any way the growth of LDCs.

Second, productivity differentials between the two countries may be higher than wage differentials. Labour content is not the same in real sense of the term even if the labour hour remains the same. For example, one hour of labour in DCs does not contain the same volume of work as one hour of labour in LDCs. It is generally pointed out that a worker in DCs is several times more productive than a worker in LDCs. This fact is well-known and has been empirically established by many studies.[17] Since productivity is higher in DCs, the value of commodities will necessarily be lower in DCs. So terms of value wages in DCs may be lower than wages in

LDCs.[18] Thus, workers of DCs do not in any way exploit the workers of LDCs. Moreover, the advantages gained from the unequal exchange do not accrue to labour, as Emmanuel wrongly thinks; but they accrue to capital of DCs.[19]

Third, Emmanuel's method of analysis has also been found to be defective, because the method of analysis of the two branches of industries of a country has been used as a proxy for the method of analysis between two countries. In fact, production in Branch I is organised on capitalist basis; and production in Branch II is also organised on capitalist basis. The two Branches used by Emmanuel show capitalist lines of production. But when Branch II is taken as a proxy for LDCs, there is a mistake because whereas Branch II in original Marxist tradition is capitalist in nature, LDCs do not have capitalist production relations. So it is a formalistic absurdity to compare Branch II with a less developed country.[20] Moreover, G. Kay points out that such an attempt is also ahistorical in nature. Where export production in LDCs is organised on a non-capitalist basis, Emmanuel's use of the Marxian transformation analysis, which is fully applicable for developed capitalist production, is wholly preposterous.[21]

Fourth, Emmanuel's conclusion is that workers of DCs benefit from the unequal exchange. This point has been countered by Geoffrey Kay.[22] In this connection, Samir Amin observes that high wages at the centre are due to high level of development of productive forces, and because of international transfer of resources from LDCs.[23]

Fifth, Emmanuel assumes that the rate of profit in DCs and LDCs is equal. Why should the rate of profit in these two countries be equal? Other things remaining the same, cost of production in DCs will show more profit per unit of output, at least in the earlier stage of capitalism. This is so because at this stage, the capitalist countries will be able to reap many external and internal economies along with increasing rate of returns, as a result of which cost of production will come down. Once we assume higher profit either as a result of lower cost or higher mark-up, that would be another source of unequal exchange not elaborated by Emmanuel. In fact, if profit rates are equalised between rich and poor countries, that can be done by the rapid growth of capitalism in LDCs. This should not only eliminate wage differentials but also would ensure faster rate of growth. But all these had not happened in LDCs. Under such a situation, the assumption of equality of profit rate seems to be based on feather-bedding arguments.

The keystone of the theory of unequal exchange is that profit rates in the absence of trade is higher in LDCs. But if the elements of constant capital are not traded, they would be cheaper in DCs. In fact, if the elements of constant capital are not traded, the LDCs will have to incur higher cost on these elements, and in that case, the profit level of LDCs will go down. So in the absence of trade, we cannot logically conclude that profit rate would be higher in LDCs. In fact, if there is trade, profit rate would be higher, and if there is no trade, profit rate of LDCs would be lower. Thus, there seems to be an internal contradiction in the theory of unequal exchange which says that trade will equalise the profit rate.[24] Trade will, on the other hand, increase the profit rate in LDCs.

In this connection, we should also note that the process which equalises rate of profit will also equalise prices. In such a case, there would hardly be any unequal exchange in the real sense between DCs and LDCs. If profit rates and prices are equal internationally, and other costs are the same, then, there would be no basis for unequal exchange.

Sixth, A. D. January and F. Kramer observe that capital mobility as assumed by Emmanuel will tend to eliminate wage differentials.[25] In that case, the theory falls to the ground.

Seventh, if the basis of unequal exchange is the wage differentials, then there can be unequal exchanges between many DCs because there are wage differentials among the DCs.[26] It is not clear how it can be the exclusive characteristic of trade between DCs and LDCs. In other words, it cannot be said that unequal exchange happens only between DCs and LDCs. Thus, it cannot be a conclusive cause for underdevelopment of LDCs.

Eighth, if the productivity in the centre is greater than that of the periphery, the higher wages existing in the centre are justified, and the theory of unequal exchange loses much of its force and rationale. It has been pointed out by critics that productivity in DCs is much higher than the productivity in LDCs, and the wage level in DCs is quite commensurate with the level of marginal productivity of labour, because in a capitalist type of firm, wage is determined by the marginal productivity of labour and it is equal to the wage rate.

Ninth, Samir Amin has pointed out that there are mainly two major errors in Emmanuel's theory of unequal exchange.[27] (i) Emmanuel wrongly treated wages as an independent variable, autonomously determined in each economy, instead of analysing wages in terms of dialectic between the laws of accumulation (objective forces) and the class struggle (subjective forces). (ii) Emmanuel has treated exports from the periphery as something specific, thus, separating the analysis of exchange from the analysis of production.

Finally, Emmanuel's analysis ignores the primary contradiction in the Third World by ignoring class struggle in LDCs. Bettelheim argues that it is only through class struggle that radical changes in production relations occur.[28] It is necessary to understand and analyse the nature of class struggles and class relations in LDCs, because these things are influencing production to a considerable extent.

However, Emmanuel makes it clear that his book deals with two independent issues. The first is the interaction of profit rate and the international division of labour which concerns the neo-Ricardians. The second is the terms of trade effect of international equalisation of profit rates. Although Emmanuel's theory is said to be a minor intellectual curiosity, his basic contribution lies in analysing the surplus extraction from the backward countries a la dependency paradigm through the application of Marxian analytical apparatus. He is perhaps the first economist who has demonstrated surplus loss and underdevelopment through trade explanation by invoking Marxian value analysis.

Notes

1. Raul Prebisch, "Commercial Policies in Underdeveloped Countries", *American Economic Review*, 1959.
2. H. Singer, "The Distribution of Gains between Investing and Borrowing Countries", *American Economic Review*, May 1950.
3. For some of the assumptions, see, Kaushik Basu, *The Less Developed Economy*, Oxford University Press, 1985, p. 54. Basu has, however, delineated only the first three assumptions.
4. Raul Prebisch, *Economic Development in Latin America and its Principal Problems*, UN Department of Economic Affairs, Lake Success, New York, 1950, p. 12.
5. Ibid. Prebisch also maintains that the economic activities of LDCs are dominated by the cycles of industrial activities in DCs.
6. H. Singer, *Op. Cit.*
7. J. N. Bhagwati, "Immiserising Growth", *Review of Economic Studies*, 1958. Bhagwati has discussed in details the effect of foreign trade on the immiserising growth of LDCs in the article.
8. Kaushik Basu, *Op. Cit.*, p. 55.
9. Tom Bottomore, *Dictionary of Marxist Thought*, Oxford University Press, London, 1983, p. 500.
10. *Loc. Cit.*
11. Geoffrey Kay, *Development and Underdevelopment*, Macmillan, London, 1975, p. 112 (Table 3). The Table and its explanation are adapted from Kay's book.
12. Ibid., p. 111.
13. Ibid., p. 113.

14. Ibid., see, for the broad interpretation of unequal exchange, G. Kay's book (Table 4). Our Table 2 is adapted from this book after making necessary corrections in (4) Table of Kay's book (p. 114).

15. Keith Griffin and John Gurley, "Radical Analyses of Imperialism, The Third World, and the Transition to Socialism: A Survey Article", *Journal of Economic Literature*, Sept. 1985, p. 1114.

16. See, C. Bettelheim's Appendix to A. A. Emmanuel's *Unequal Exchange*, Monthly Review Press, New York, 1972.

17. See, among others, W. Leontief, *Domestic Production and Foreign Trade*, Proceedings of American Philosophical Society, IF No. 4, p. 332.

18. G. Kay, *Op. Cit.*, pp. 108-18.

19. *Loc. Cit.*

20. *Loc. Cit.*

21. G. Kay *Op. Cit.*, p. 119.

22. G. Kay, *Op. Cit.*, p. 108, Kay observes that capital is benefitted by unequal exchange and not labour.

23. S. Amin, *Imperialism and Unequal Development*, Harvester Press, Sussex, 1977, p. 222.

24. E. Dore and J. Weeks, "International Exchange and Causes of Backwardness", *Latin American Perspective*, 1977.

25. A. D. Janvry and F. Kramer, "Limits of Unequal Exchange", *Review of Radical Political Economics*, Winter 1979, p. 30. This point has been countered by Bill Gibson. See, Bill Gibson, "Unequal Exchange: Theoretical Issues and Empirical Findings", *Review of Radical Political Economics*, Fall 1980.

26. S. Smith, "The Ideas of Samir Amin: Theory or Tautology?", *Journal of Development Studies*, Oct. 1980. The point is raised by S. Smith in discussing Amin's ideas on unequal exchange.

27. S. Amin, *Op. Cit.*, p. 221.

28. C. Bettelheim, *Op. Cit.*

8 The Peripheral Writers on Dependency

In the earlier sections, I have analysed the contributions of many important dependency writers. However, I could not discuss all the writers of this school of economic thought. There are many writers in the dependency school, such as P.O. Brien, Stein and Stein, Robert Brenner, Immanuel Wallerstein, Celso Furtado, O. Sunkel, F. H. Cardoso, G. Kay, Bill Warren and others. Since it is not possible to analyse the contributions of all these writers here, I will concentrate on a few of them for the purpose of the present analysis. The theory of dependency has not evoked same and similar responses from all scholars of the subject. While some have analysed and extended the theory of dependency, others have gone against this paradigm. I have chosen here some writers who have made their marks in this area of research.

Furtado finds the explanation of underdevelopment in the dualism that is created as a result of capitalist penetration in the less developed countries. The capitalist structure which is already developed cannot be properly linked with the archaic domestic economic structure. According to Furtado, underdevelopment is not a necessary stage in the process of formation of the modern capitalist economy. He begins with the structure of the world economy as a totality within which underdeveloped countries are subsystems, and so the theory of underdevelopment turns out essentially to be a theory of dependence. Geoffrey Kay's position is somewhat different. He observes that in the absence of the Marxian analysis of value as the theoretical *terra firma*, dependency theory has degenerated into hopeless contradiction in the face of historical categories, although it could give a historical account of the process of underdevelopment. According to him, the radical theory of dependency could not capture the real issue which is: capital created underdevelopment not because it exploited the underdeveloped world, but because it did not exploit enough.

F. H. Cardoso observes that dependency is congenial and not inimical to development. In fact, foreign capital has been helping the industrialisation process in many LDCs. Likewise, Warren asserts that capitalism and imperialism have been responsible for various types of development in LDCs. Dependency, according to him is necessary for economic development. Cardoso and Warren have criticised the theory of dependency by saying that dependency theorists could not understand the proper far-reaching roles of dependency on economic development of LDCs. Under many situations, central capitalism has helped the developing countries. Osvaldo Sunkel accepts the truth-value of the theory of dependency, but rather than giving it a rigorous analytical exposition, he outlines the national policy of development which can overcome dependency in Latin American countries. According to him, national development policy requires substantial readjustment in domestic development strategy. In order to overcome dependence, it is necessary to have the transformation of the internal structure of production and to have some change in the nature of foreign ties. Without the structural transformation and changes in the nature of foreign relations, dependency can never be eliminated. The capitalist sector can peacefully co-exist with the traditional sector. But when the capitalist sector absorbs a large number of local wage earners, it can have some effects on the local economy. It needs to be remembered that all hybrid economies do not behave in the same way. For instance, the behaviour of Brazil was different from that of other dependent countries. As a result of capitalist penetration, there may be substantial growth of the monetary sector. This can make substantial modifications in the consumption habits of the local people, which may lead to the introduction of many manufactured articles from abroad. The diversification in consumption habits has had important consequences on the subsequent development of the native economy.

(A) Celso Furtado on Underdevelopment and Dualism

The dependent economy may be inter-linked with the foreign capitalist sector. In simple underdeveloped structure, the mass of the wages generated in the exporting sector becomes a dynamic element. But in the more complex underdeveloped structure where the industrial nucleus is linked with the domestic market, there may be a tendency for the structural transformation of the system. In such a case, the basic dynamic factor is the external demand. A higher stage in underdevelopment is achieved when the industrial nucleus becomes diversified and is able to produce part of the equipment needed for the expansion of productive forces.

Furtado believes that underdevelopment is not a necessary stage in the process of formation of the modern capitalistic economies. The phenomenon of underdevelopment has a number of dimensions. In the simplest case, there may be the co-existence of foreign companies producing export commodities along with a wide range of subsistence activities. In a backward country, there may be the presence of three sectors: a subsistence structure, a structure oriented towards mainly export, and an industrial nucleus connected with the domestic market and sufficiently diversified to produce a part of the required capital goods.

Furtado defines underdeveloped structure as one in which full utilisation of available capital is not a sufficient condition for complete absorption of the working force at a level of productivity corresponding to the technology prevailing in the dynamic sector of the economy.[1] Underdevelopment is mainly characterised by the technological heterogeneity of the various sectors of the economy. Technology, in fact, is an independent variable. Underdevelopment is regarded by Furtado as a state of factor imbalance reflecting a lack of adjustment between the availability of factors and the technology for their use. This imbalance does not permit full utilisation of the given factors of production. The degree of the underdevelopment is a function of the relative importance of the backward sector, and the rate of growth is a function of the increase in the relative importance of the developed sector which has been incorporated from outside.[2] Growth mainly depends on the rate of population growth. Furtado observes that despite the rise in per capita income, the degree of underdevelopment is not altered comparably.[3] The growth of an underdeveloped economy, Furtado believes, implies structural modification.

In underdeveloped economies that have achieved some degree of diversification in their production structures, a dynamic impulse does induce a stage of rapid economic growth. It is a general feature of an underdeveloped economy that its capital formation process depends greatly on foreign trade. While the formation of savings becomes less dependent on the export sector, the transformation of savings into real capital involves greater dependency.

The difference between developed and underdeveloped economies stems from the global process of resource allocation and the structuring of the world economy.[4] When certain countries became peripheral, they were transformed into importers of new consumer goods from abroad. The penetration of capitalist system into backward countries changed the pattern of consumption of a particular section of the people of the backward country. Furtado traces the cultural dependence of the periphery to the activities of the centre associated with the stimulus provided to the conclaves of the peripheries. Furtado believes that the opportunities offered by static comparative advantages of conclave patterns of development create cultural domination through the continuous satisfaction of the demands of small elite groups having different values than the masses of the periphery. A small number of people imitate the consumption pattern of the DCs. This can be a factor in the transformation of the peripheral countries. To increase consumption of rich people means to introduce new products, and this implies expansion in different directions and a change in the pattern of the productive system.

The process of introduction of the consumption pattern of DCs in LDCs gave rise to peripheral capitalism. This capitalism is unable to generate innovations and is dependent on the decision coming from foreign capitalism. Furtado says that external dependence is a structural situation in which peripheral capitalism prevails in some countries where modernisation was started on the basis of static comparative advantage and has operated as a framework for the process of cultural domination. Once this dependence has been created, all types of economic exploitations can be practised in such countries. The developed capitalist countries influence the consumption pattern and the technology of the dependent countries. This may lead to the growth of technological colonialism. Underdevelopment implies the inability of the economic system to spontaneously generate the demand profile required to assure the growth of the industrial sector linked to the modernised minority.[5] The present growth of the dependent economies consists of increasing participation on the part of multinational corporations (MNCs). MNCs provide new products and may play the role of an engine of growth in LDCs while maintaining the tight links of dependence.[6] MNCs, however, take the benefit of increased productivity in LDCs.

In the course of economic development of LDCs, there may be disequilibrium because of insufficiency of comparable production in some lines whereas there may be over-production in some other lines. Any attempt at increasing investment rate without proper orientation of the new resources invested may create internal disequilibrium between demand and supply. This disequilibrium may be transferred to the balance of payments. However, elimination of internal and external disequilibrium will require careful investment guidance. If there is a rise in the import co-efficient in the early stage of development, there may be balance of payments disequilibrium. Such disequilibrium may also be caused by internal inflation. However, devaluation under such a situation will be harmful because it will reduce the actual rate of economic growth by raising the prices of capital goods. In many cases, the disequilibrium may be corrected by reducing the level of expenditure and also by external over-valuation of the currency. In any case, it is necessary to make sure that investment will produce the structural changes favourable for economic development. Without a particular type of structural changes, economic development is not possible.

According to Furtado, development process involves either new combination of existing factors at a given technical level or the introduction of technical innovations. LDCs do not have the improved technology. In LDCs, there is always underutilisation of factors of production. Underutilisation, however, does not necessarily arise from faulty combination of existing factors. Rather, it results from scarcity of capital which also leads to under utilisation of man-power. Moreover, the average productivity of the combined factors is also much lower in LDCs. This is partly because of the rigidity of technical co-efficients of factors of production. Introduction of new technology can always increase productivity in LDCs. Economic development consists of the introduction of new combination of factors which tends to increase labour productivity. The increase in productivity leads to a rise in the real income, and the resultant increase in demand leads to changes in the composition of demand and also in the structure of production. The basic obstacle in the way of economic development in LDCs is the lowest level of productivity. Once the process of growth starts, a part of the increased income can be allocated for capital formation. However, it is very difficult for the backward countries to set the process of development by their own means.

Economic development involves increasingly capitalistic processes. As productivity grows, real income also grows and demand becomes more diversified, so that new opportunities are opened up for further investment. Economic development, after all, is a process of capital accumulation. The way demand develops is a basic determinant of the course of new investment which is the building block of economic development.

The development of industrial nucleus in the eighteenth century in Europe affected the development process of almost every region of the world. When this industrial capitalism was introduced in the densely

106

populated backward regions, it influenced the pre-capitalist system and perpetuated it. The capitalist penetration created a structural dualism which characterises the present-day Third World countries. These countries have become dependent on the developed industrial countries of the world. And unless the structures of these countries are completely changed, there cannot be any economic development in these countries in the true sense of the term.

(B) Geoffrey Kay's Views on Development and Underdevelopment

Geoffrey Kay starts his analysis as a critique of both the *theory of dependency* and the *theory of unequal exchange*. According to Kay, these phenomena are typical of merchant capitalism when merchant capitalism exists in an independent form. Merchant capitalism cannot transform the mode of production. According to Kay, the main cause of underdevelopment of the periphery is the inability of the merchant capitalism to transform into industrial capitalism.[7] There are a few important characteristics of merchant capitalism. These are listed below:

(a)   Merchant capitalism existed much earlier than industrial capitalism

(b)   It works in the circulation sphere

(c)   It has no control over the labour process, i.e. it cannot influence labour productivity

(d)   Merchant capitalism depends on the class which exploits labour and it supports that class

(e)   The surplus value that is accumulated by merchant capitalism is used for the expansion of trade and not for the expansion of industry (Kay, pp. 86-95)

(f)   Merchant capitalism became the agent of industrial capitalism in course of time.

By itself, merchant capitalism is unable to initiate a process of industrial development in LDCs. This itself created a structure of underdevelopment. At certain stage, merchant capitalism was forced to start production but it could not encourage the process of industrialisation in LDCs and it was not able to establish capitalist mode of production.

Geoffrey Kay has pointed out that none of the earlier neo-Marxist theories of development and underdevelopment is based on the Marxian theory of value. Kay observes that the phenomenon of development/underdevelopment can better be explained with reference to Marx's labour theory of value and the historical role of merchant capitalism and industrial capitalism. Kay is of the opinion that because of the existence of merchant capitalism in LDCs, growth process could not be initiated there.

After all, economic development is a historical process which has specific social, economic and political milieu. The root of the problem associated with development and underdevelopment is to be found in the relations of production. According to Kay, the writers of the dependency school do not use the classical Marxist theory of value. Kay believes that a satisfactory theory of underdevelopment must be based on the law of value.

In LDCs, capital is first introduced in the form of merchant capital. This type of capital participates in the process of exchange. It makes a two-fold profit. *One,* it buys from the native producers and sells the commodities to the developed countries or to productive capital. *Second*, it buys from the DCs and sells the same commodities to the LDCs. In both these cases, the merchant capital accumulates surplus because the sale is at higher prices than the purchase. Thus, it is in trade where the wealth or capital of a merchant is always utilised. The circuit of capital is the value in motion and the pursuit of pure quantity. This type of capital is the typical feature of less developed countries. The introduction of industrial capital which is essential for starting the growth process is a very complex one, and it cannot be practically made possible so easily in LDCs.

It should be noted that in order to gather surplus, the merchant capital must engage itself in *unequal exchange*. Merchant capital by itself cannot increase the values of those commodities which it deals in. This is consistent with the law of value that is applicable to the merchant capital. A merchant capital also appropriates the surplus value from out of the finance capital that may also appear side by side with the merchant capital. Merchant capital has no direct control over the labour process, i.e. wage determination and surplus value creation. Therefore, such capital has to depend on the producers' class. Merchant capital started in Britain long before the start of industrial capitalism. In fact, industrial capitalism started in Britain at the end of the eighteenth century, but merchant capitalism had already started nearly two and a half centuries prior to this. Merchant capital exploited and destroyed many parts of the world through its process of accumulation of surplus. This surplus was mostly used for the expansion of trade and not for the forces of production. In other words, the surplus value was always utilised in the sphere of circulation. However, merchant capital did give some encouragement to commodity production. Thus, we have side by side a contradictory role of merchant capital as both a stimulant and an obstacle for the development of the forces of production. Merchant capital opened and at the same time blocked the way for the full development of capitalism. Indeed, merchant capital did start in many LDCs' new commercial and educational centres for the benefit of the people.

However, with the growth of industrial capitalism after the industrial revolution, two important changes took place in the world. *First*, the division of labour was extended and became institutionalised in many countries, and *second*, the profit of merchant capital began to reduce. The world was divided on the basis of the new division of labour as the primary producing countries and the industrial economies. The increased division of labour not only increased production and productivity but it also extended the scope for increased exploitation, and a new foundation for development and underdevelopment was established.

With the coming of industrial revolution, the industrial capital established its hegemony and several consequences followed: *Firstly*, the profit of the merchant capital was reduced. *Secondly*, the world was divided into two groups – agricultural countries and industrial countries. *Thirdly*, merchant capital's monopolistic advantages were destroyed. *Fourthly*, merchant capital formed a part of industrial capital, and *Lastly*, merchant capital was forced to be an agent of industrial capital. As a matter of fact, merchant capital at some places retained its independent status, but at the same time, it became the agent of industrial capital. This two-fold character is supposed by some radical development economists as the economics of dependency. But Kay observes that this concept fails to grasp the real meaning and nature of the process of underdevelopment in the less developed countries.[8]

Confronted with the situation of falling profit, merchant capital tried to increase its control over the market. In many respects, merchant capital opened the way for industrial capitalism but at the same time, it hindered its actual progress. Be that as it may, the introduction of industrial capital strengthened the structure of underdevelopment in many ways. Merchant capital in non-capitalist countries existed as the single independent type of capital; but in capitalist countries, it worked as a part of industrial capital, and after the industrial revolution, it completely merged with industrial capital.

For many reasons, industrial capitalism could not be started in LDCs. Moreover, industrial capital was also not interested in introducing industrial capitalism in such countries. This is so because industrial capital considered LDCs as a source for the cheap raw materials and also as a market for the sale of finished goods. However, the merchant capital in such countries became the agent of industrial capital. After the establishment industrial capitalism in DCs, merchant capital retained its two historical forms at the same: it was the only form of capital and at the same time, it was not really the only form of capital. According to Kay, this apparent paradox is the *differentia specificia* of underdevelopment, and its emergence as a historical fact in the course of the nineteenth century marks the beginning of underdevelopment as we know it today.[9]

Merchant capital made profit by selling agricultural commodities abroad and industrial commodities in LDCs. But its ability to make profits sufficiently declined after the introduction of industrial capitalism. Its role was now subordinated to industrial capital. But still, it made profits through unequal exchange. However, it could not practise exploitation beyond a point. Moreover, it had no power to increase labour productivity. Labour productivity could be increased by industrial capital through the introduction of better technique of production. Thus, as a result of competition, merchant capitalism faced a sort of crisis. And by the beginning of the twentieth century, merchant capital began to lose its independence. Then, it was forced to act as productive capital openly. Thus, there was an attempt to introduce capitalist mode of production in LDCs. But the conditions in LDCs were entirely different than those in DCs. Therefore, industrialisation did not follow the same path in LDCs as it followed in DCs. There could not be the total transformation of the economy and the society. The industrial development in LDCs and in DCs followed structurally dissimilar patterns. Industrialisation in LDCs was uneven, partial and capital-intensive in nature. Capital intensity created large amounts of unemployment in such countries. The attempt to have industrialisation took place under conditions of deeply established milieu of underdevelopment which could not be really overcome, but the tendency became reinforced. Thus, underdevelopment perpetuated.

A new phase started since the depression of the Thirties. During this period, the profit of the merchant capital significantly reduced. Moreover, in many LDCs, nationalist movement gained momentum and industrial production centres began to be established. The merchant capital still played its dual role. Industrialisation started feebly. But this was neither the solution to the problem of underdevelopment nor the beginning of economic development. This type of nascent industrialisation could not solve the problem of unemployment, but it concentrated on the development of a few primary processing centres for the purpose of export and on some import substitution activities. The industrialisation was lopsided and incomplete. The mode of production could not be completely changed.

Kay observes that the concept of dependency fails to grasp the real nature of the process of underdevelopment. In the absence of an analysis based on law of value, the dependency analysis gives rise to categories such as periphery, metropole, dependency and so on, which collapse into hopeless contradiction in the face of investigation. In fact, the radical writers on dependency failed to pin-point the crucial issue that capital created under-development not because it exploited the underdeveloped world, but because it did not exploit it enough.[10]

(C) F.H. Cardoso on Dependency and Development in Latin America

F. H. Cardoso has given some new ideas on the theory of dependency. His ideas are entirely different from the ideas which were prevalent earlier. He has criticised the existing theories of dependency in a systematic manner. He has pointed out that there are the following main inter-connected wrong notions of the theories of dependency.[11] These five common notions are:

(i)   Capitalist development in Latin America does not seem to be possible

(ii)   Local bourgeoisies no longer exist as an active social and dynamic force for economic development

(iii)   Dependent capitalism is based on the extensive exploitation of labour which implies that labour is not paid the justified wage. The actual wage level is lower than the warranted wage level. Therefore, there is the exploitation of labour

(iv)   The multinational corporations force the domestic state to follow a sub-imperialist policy

(v)   The only political action that can be taken to eliminate the existing disorder is to take resort to socialism or fascism.

All these common elements of the theory of the dependency have been rejected one by one by F.H. Cardoso. Cardoso has observed that with the change in the world capitalist system, the centre-periphery relation has also considerably changed. He is of the opinion that foreign capital has been mainly directed for the development of manufacturing industry in the periphery. Such foreign capital is not harmful for the satellite countries. On the other hand, the main aim of foreign capital is to help in the development process of the peripheral countries. In this sense, Cardoso does not find any contradiction between dependency and industrialisation of the developing countries. On the other hand, Cardoso thinks that dependency can be helpful for the process of industrial development in LDCs. He also feels that the political, social and economic processes in LDCs which are dependent societies can be explained by the specificity of movement there, as a dialectic unity of both *internal* and *external* forces. As a matter of fact, the external domination can reappear as an internal phenomenon through the practices and cultures of local classes and groups who share the mutual interests and values of the society, while others may oppose the foreign capitalist domination. The domination may be liked by some, and may be disliked by others. Therefore, there can be a contradiction of opinions and values, out of which there can be the emergence of a new type of thinking. There will ultimately generate in a dialectical way a new type of dynamic society. Thus, according to Cardoso, it is not true to say that one type of world capitalist system is producing underdevelopment and external forces combine into a very complicated type of relationship which determines ultimately the final shape of the society to come.

Cardoso puts forward a new type of arguments which looks at the dependency theory as something congenial to and not opposed to economic development of the peripheral countries. He has popularised the idea of "associated dependent development" to elaborate his thesis. Dependency and development are positively correlated. This, however, goes against the traditional notion of dependency theory which upholds that dependency invariably leads to underdevelopment. In the dependent type of capitalist development, as is found in Latin American countries, there takes place, according to Cardoso, some internal structural fragmentation. In the course of this structural change many classes in the society like the bourgeoisie, middle class and a part of the working class do become the real beneficiaries. The classes which are employed by the internationalised sector do really enjoy some extra benefits.

According to Cardoso, changes in international capitalist organisation as represented by the multinational corporations (MNCs), have produced a new type of division of labour. Cardoso argues that in many ways, the MNCs are responsible for the internal development of dependent countries. He observes that it is actually not true to say that MNCs simply extract surpluses from LDCs and perpetuate their state of underdevelopment. The traditional view that MNCs are agents of economic imperialism does no longer seem to be true. The attitude towards MNCs needs to be reformulated. Through massive foreign investment, the MNCs try to supply finished manufactured goods for satisfying the growing needs of different classes of people in the dependent country. As a matter of fact, rapid economic growth of some crucial sectors of the dependent country does very much depend on the MNCs. It is, thus, clear that Cardoso's notion of dependency is diametrically opposed to the notion of classical dependency approach.

(D) Bill Warren's Views on Dependency

Bill Warren considers that imperialist penetration has indeed brought about whatever development exists in the less developed countries.[12] He is also in favour of keeping a close contact between LDCs and DCs for the economic development of the former group of countries. In a dependent type of relation, the rate of growth of LDCs depends on the rate of growth of the advanced countries.

Warren observes that dependency is a complex type of politico-economic relationship that binds the DCs of the centre with the LDCs in such a way that the movements and structure of the former decisively determine those of the latter in a fashion which is detrimental to the economic progress of the peripheral countries. But there is a conceptual problem of knowing the correct connotation of the concept *detrimental*. The problem originates in the nationalist policy pursued by the dependency school. This school has its utopian criterion of *national development*. However, this concept itself can be interpreted in so many ways depending on the subjective attitude of the analyst.[13]

According to him, dependency theorists generally equate imperialism with the world market. They, thus, conclude by definition the possibility of any non-dependent third world capitalist development. This is not correct, according to Bill Warren. Warren believes that imperialism must and does actually carry out the task of development.[14] Warren defends the role of capitalism in LDCs. His main objective is to revive the classical Marxist perspective on capitalism. His work is a formidable attack on the nationalist tendency in neo-Marxism. The allegation that neo-Marxism is based on a confusion between anti-imperialism and anti-capitalism is a constant theme in his critique against dependency theory. According to Warren, capital provides dynamic thrust to economic development. Warren argues that the bulk of current Marxist analysis and propaganda about imperialism reverses the views of the founders of Marxism, who held that the expansion of capitalism into the pre-capitalist areas of the world was desirable and progressive. The reversal of Marxist view is based on the theory of the advent of a new and degenerate stage of monopoly capitalism which cannot perform any longer any positive social function. This idea was prevalent in Lenin's theory of imperialism; but later on, it became a dogma. According to this dogma, imperialism came to be regarded as the major obstacle to development. This notion was then generalised and capitalism began to be regarded as retrogressive system. This type of shift in the Marxian theory was completed in 1928 at the Congress of the Comintern. The inherent logic of anti-imperialist nationalism was that more rapid and extensive development of capitalism was not properly understood by the nationalists and Marxists. However, Warren could accept nationalism without any difficulty if capitalism could be taken as desirable and progressive.

Warren thought that third world countries were rapidly developing either independently of imperial centres, or because of imperial centres, or despite imperial domination. However, in his later work, Warren conflated imperialism with capitalism and extended the classical Marxist perspective on capitalism to imperialism. He defines imperialism as "...penetration and spread of the capitalist system into non-capitalist or primitive capitalist areas of the world....". Since Marx considered the role of capitalism in pre-capitalist societies as progressive, Warren thought that people should welcome the extension of capitalism to the less developed countries. He argues for the existence of a unitary process of imperialist-induced development. Warren considers successful capitalist development as that development which provides the appropriate economic, social and political conditions for the continuing reproduction of capital as a social system, and not as the adequacy of development as a process of satisfying the basic needs of the people.

Warren goes on to add that in any reasonable historical perspective, capitalism has steadily devoted greater and greater proportions of its resources to public welfare. According to him, in the case of India of the colonial time, capitalism, far from initiating a reinforcing process of underdevelopment, started almost from the beginning, a process of development in terms of improvements in material and better conditions for the development of the productive forces.[15]

Both Lenin's theory and dependency theory of underdevelopment consider imperialism and capitalism as retrogressive in character, whereas, according to Warren, these are progressive in nature. It should be noted that Warren evaluates capitalism and imperialism with reference to the productive forces. Warren finds precisely that capitalist exploitation is legitimate. He observes that it is not necessary to fight against imperialism because it helps to spread capitalism, and capitalism is appropriate for economic growth.

Warren attaches much significance to the growth of productive forces. He, however, considers capitalism as an abstract process rather than a specific mode of production. But he does not make reference to the classes and the class struggles. If we consider capitalism as an abstract process, we really produce a Hegelian rather than a Marxian version of history. Warren's analysis fails to account for the differentiation between, and the specification of, the development experience of the third world countries.

However, from his analysis, it becomes clear that like Samir Amin, Warren has also interpreted capitalism with reference to the development of the productive forces. Moreover, both these scholars were pre-occupied with the relation between capitalism and development as an abstract process, considering a unitary version of an all-or-nothing polarity. But both the writers fail to take account of the historical significance of the third world countries. Warren is of the opinion that dependency school of thought is unable to provide any valid prescription to ward off dependency from the LDCs. This is so because, as Warren believes, the school is based on subjective and moralistic criteria. Warren's analysis provides a critique against the dependency school of development and underdevelopment.

(E) Osvaldo Sunkel on External Dependence and National Development Policy

Sunkel regards development as a global structural process of change. According to him, LDCs are those countries which lack an autonomous capacity for change and growth and, are dependent on the centre. The objectives , intensity, instruments and efficiency of development policies are limited within certain margins of flexibility.[16] Sunkel considers certain structural features of LDCs as responsible for their underdevelopment. He observes that some of these structural traits can be attributed to the relationship between LDCs and DCs. In an adequate historical perspective, development appears as a process of transformation of economic, social, political and cultural structures and institutions.[17]

Sunkel thinks that the spread of capitalism in dependent countries is responsible for national as well as international inequalities. He observes that development and underdevelopment are the two faces of the universal process, and that its geographical expression is given in the form of two great polarisations. On the one hand, there is polarisation of the world between industrial, developed and advanced metropolitan countries, and on the other, we have poor, backward, peripheral and dependent countries. Moreover, there may be polarisation even inside the countries in terms of space, groups and activities.

While analysing the relations of dependence and interdependence between LDCs and DCs, Sunkel points out that the nature of development process of the periphery would become induced by the autonomous development process of the centre. However, this factor was absent during the development process of the present day developed countries. The influence which external relations exercise on the national development policy derives from the fact that the Latin American countries are having dependent relationship with capitalist world. The study of conventional development policies reveals the existence of many contradictory tendencies, some of which reinforce dependency but others may provide some scope for a policy towards greater independence. In Latin America, there are interest groups and sectors associated with foreign activities, as well as tendencies towards cultural and ideological alienation which hinder the transformations implicit in any national development programme.[18]

Industrialisation in Latin America has not produced all the expected benefits; in particular, it has not resulted in the lessening of dependence on foreign countries. The policy of import substitution has resulted in great vulnerability of the balance of payments and also in foreign financial commitments which in some Latin American countries represent a considerable size of foreign exchange reserves.

Sunkel has elaborated many characteristic processes of the national economy, like the stagnation of traditional agriculture, the structure of foreign trade, limited industrialisation and the limited function of the state. The Latin American countries are entirely dependent on foreign economic relations with respect to the structure and function of the economy. This extreme dependence is rooted in several conditions, such as the vulnerability and structural deficit of the balance of payments, and the exploitation of the export sector. All these have created conditions which have not helped the Latin American countries to adapt and create their own technology. Foreign financing means the accumulation of considerable debts the servicing of which requires additional foreign financing. All this creates a genuine vicious circle. Because of the dire necessity of foreign financing, the condition of foreign independence has become very essential. But the tragedy is that the LDCs do not get the entire requirements of foreign resources from the DCs, *Secondly*, the import substitution which has become a method of industrialisation in recent years tends to stagnate. Dependency is structurally inherent in all LDCs. In order to be genuine, development must tend to replace dependence with interdependence, *i.e.* a situation in which the nation has to confront outside pressures or limitations. These may create possibilities for alternative choices.

Sunkel argues that to overcome dependency, it is necessary to transform existing structure in order to create a capacity for autonomous growth. To have growth, one must be able to manipulate natural, technical and social factors as well as relations with other countries in the pursuit of economic development.

In this context, the necessity of Latin American integration acquires a special meaning. Integration can be either a basic instrument of national realisation, or can be the instrument of accelerated dependence. However, the present condition and policies favour the latter tendency.[19] The multinational corporations working in Latin America try to displace the national industries even in the domestic market. Sunkel observes that multinational corporations introduce a dependent type of technology and monopolistic practices in the factors and the product markets, and transfer surplus from Latin American countries and introduce the consumption pattern of the DCs. The tastes and preferences for durable consumer goods of the DCs, necessitate imports, and the dependence continues. In order to sever the links with the MNCs, it would be necessary to have our own capacity of technological creation, large scale production in sectors with high and increasing productivity and to develop sectors which can create sufficient resources.[20] In other words, the immediate efforts for integration must be concentrated on the establishment of production agreements with the Latin American enterprises or consortiums.

National development policy demands substantial readjustments in domestic development strategy. Foreign aid must be used with caution because the aid money may be misused. It is necessary to overcome dependence. For this, it is essential to have the transformation of the internal structure of production and to have some change in the nature of foreign ties. If this is achieved, then foreign help can yield real fruits. But without the structural transformation and changes in the nature of foreign relations, there would be more dependence.

But how to have the internal structural change? Sunkel says that the structural changes must be carried out in all the sectors of the economy. In agriculture, it is necessary to increase the growth of agricultural production so that it can be made available at lower relative prices to the other sectors. It should also create substantial export surplus. This may, alongwith import substitution, diminish foreign dependence. Agrarian reforms must fulfil the general objectives of agrarian policy and national development.

In the field of foreign trade, Sunkel advises to increase export and to diversify the entire field of export. It is also important to have import substitution. Export must not only increase, it must also be diversified. Exporting countries must seek international cooperation among the developing countries so that they can negotiate with DCs on better terms. These cooperations may also result in the improvement of terms of trade which can transfer some resources from the DCs.

Domestically, more and more development-oriented policies must be formulated. It is necessary to collect basic information regarding all sectors of the economy, and to have special control over the export sector. The introduction of technological improvement is absolutely fundamental for determining the dynamic comparative advantages. It is not only essential to exploit the resources but also to use them in optimum manner. It will be necessary to modify or replace the traditional forms of incorporating modern technology.

The concept of industrial co-operation will open the doors to new ways of association with private foreign enterprises which may be helpful to overcome many disadvantages and achieve some advantages of foreign private enterprises. Regarding technology, Sunkel advises to follow a restrictive policy which will help the utilisation of the idle capacity already existing in the economy. He also favours the idea of having industrial concentration in large specialised productive unit because it can lead to the adequate utilisation of existing capacity, increase in productivity and reduction in cost. However, there must be some form of social control over big businesses. Latin American countries should think of forming their own multinational companies and having industrial cooperation agreements with the advanced countries.

The countries of the underdeveloped regions have now greater possibilities of trade, aid and technical assistance with other fellow-developing countries. In fact, contacts among LDCs are expanding very rapidly now. This can put the DCs to some inconvenience because the LDCs can cooperate among themselves for mutual help. This can give the possibility of less dependence on the DCs.

Sunkel summarises the discussion by pointing out that national development should be the fundamental objective. *Second*, the reduction of external dependence requires very important re-orientation in traditional development strategy, specially with respect to agriculture, integration, foreign relation and industrial policy. *Third*, there are many possibilities for formulation and application of new policies on the basis of mutual cooperation among the LDCs. *Lastly*, certain changes in the international situation have created conditions which are congenial and flexible for the formulation and implementation of national development policy.

(F) Immanuel Wallerstein's Modern World System

The creation of modern world is a great watershed in history. Wallerstein has tried to study the development pattern of the modern world system (MWS). MWS is a unidimensional system. It is essentially a social system.[21] In Wallerstein's analysis, sixteenth century is the mainspring of the MWS because without the thrust of the sixteenth century, the modern world could not have emerged. The modern world system is marked by dialectical forces of exploitation and refusal to accept exploitation and the like, but the climax has not yet reached. The MWS is a self-contained economic entity based on extensive divisions of labour. The MWS contains a multiplicity of cultures and political arrangements.

According to Wallterstein, there existed so far mainly two varieties of world system: (i) world empires, and (ii) world economy. However, in the past, world economies had highly unstable structure. But the modern world economy has survived for many hundred years and has not been converted to world empires. The main source of strength to the modern world economy is the economic organisation, called *capitalism*. Under capitalism, economic factors operate within an arena larger than that which any political entity can totally control.[22] Capitalism has freedom of manipulation which is structurally permissible. This has made possible the expansion although with unequal distribution of rewards. He has also recognised closed *mini-systems* in the form of local economies. Wallerstein has pointed out that a socialist world government may constitute the third possible form of world system. But no such arrangement exists in the present world and it was also not present in the sixteenth century.

Be that as it may, the size of world economy is a function of the state of technology. The boundaries of world economy are ever fluid.[23] The division of labour in the world economy is not merely functional but it is also geographical. Economic functions are not evenly distributed in the world system. The social organisation of work in such a system may mean exploitation of one group and profit for the other. In the world economy, the political structure links culture with spatial location, but in world empire, it links culture with occupation. In a world economy, the first point of political pressure available to groups is the local (national) state structure.

The world economies are divided into three layers: *The core, semi-periphery and the periphery*. In the core sector, the state machinery integrates satisfactorily the national culture in such a way that a mechanism can be built up to justify and protest inequalities and disparities. Whereas the state is very strong in the core sector, it is very weak in the periphery. The semi-periphery area is created by the changing geopolitical situations of either core or periphery. The semi-periphery is a necessary intermediary and structural adjunct in the world economy. The process of development of world economy brings about technological advances which are helpful for expanding the boundaries of world economy. Wallerstein argues that technologically speaking, modern world economy is essentially a capitalist economy and it developed in the sixteenth century. Sixteenth century was the time of travail in much of Europe. It was also the era of reformation, counter-reformation and of great religious civil wars. In this century, the European world economy tended to be a one-class system.

In a world system, it is necessary to appreciate the roles of classes and status groups. According to Wallerstein, the number of *effective* classes in such a system will be reduced to only two, but there can be multitudes of occupational interest groups. However, class formation in the sixteenth century was indecisive: the capitalist class was formed but it did not triumph in the political domain.

A strong state is a partially autonomous entity and it serves the interest of some groups of people as may emerge within the framework of capitalist world economy. Whereas a strong state can coordinate a complex social industrial-commercial-agricultural mechanism, a weak state cannot do so. In MWS, the social system is built on a multiplicity of value systems within.

As a matter of fact, national homogeneity within international heterogeneity is the corner-stone of world economy.[24] Wallerstein is basically concerned with the socio-economic transformation of early modern Europe and its impact on the rest of the world. He has tried to trace the development of the modern world, or *world system* from the time the European economy first became the world economy. Wallerstein argues that three things were necessary for the establishment of a capitalist world economy.[25] *First*, expansion of Europe. *Second*, the development of different forms of labour control for different regions within the world economy, and *third*, the creation of strong state machinery in the core states. A strong state can help the transfer of surplus from periphery through various means like protectionism, restrictions, annexation by force and so on.[26]

Wallerstein makes a precise delineation of pre-capitalist and capitalist social systems. He observes that social system is of prime importance and that external factors would take precedence over the internal factors in any fruitful analysis of underdevelopment. In his analysis, the core sector (capitalist sector) with the help of strong state machinery tries to grab the surplus of the periphery and weakens the periphery. The semi-periphery is kept as a buffer. It is both an exploiter and an exploited one. The semi-periphery is vital to Wallerstein's divide-and-rule account of the failures of periphery politicisation.[27] It is to be noted that surplus transfer in the world-empire is not a problem, as it is done by force; but this not so in the world system. In Wallerstein's analysis, like Frank's, it is capitalism as a universal system which is responsible for development of underdevelopment.[28] The concept of capitalism encompasses the notion of surplus transfer from countries (peripheries) to the centre (core).

Many historians and geographers have lauded Wallerstein for his attempt to socialise the geographical imagination. However, many of his ideas are already implicit in the works of many dependency theorists, particularly Frank. Many points of criticism can be levelled against his work. Wallerstein has neglected the analysis of the concept of *class* and *class struggle*.[29] He assumes capitalist rationality before capitalism itself. This is the typical ahistorical nature of the analysis.[30] Wallerstein explains development/underdevelopment in terms of surplus transfer. However, he needs to analyse as to how the surplus is utilised for development. This requires a reference to class structure, which Wallerstein has thoroughly neglected.

Why one system? In fact, many people think that there are really many systems in the world. Indeed, it is more meaningful to consider a system with reference to or *vis-à-vis* other systems. The contrast made between *empire* and *world economy* appears to be both simplistic and over-stated.[31] The assumption of one mode of production seems to be another simplication. Braudel has questioned Wallerstein's fascination with the sixteenth century because European capitalism really started in the thirteenth century in Italy.[32] Wallerstein's theory is a one-dimensional theory of materialist fundamentalism within a centrist framework. It does not really explain adequately the theory of dependency. However, as Appleby has observed, the great value of Wallerstein's work is precisely that it has offered a paradigm of the transformation of modern capitalism. [33]

(G) Marini's Dependencia Dialectica

R. M. Marini has made a systematic attempt to lay down certain specific laws governing the dependent economies of less developed countries.[34] But unfortunately, his work has remained more or less unknown to the English-speaking world of intellectuals. Marini's fundamental thesis concerns the fact that in the dependent nations, labour is *over-exploited* or *super-exploited*.[35] But why is labour over-exploited? Marini observes that over-exploitation of labour in the periphery is needed by capitalists to partially compensate for the falling rate of profit that arises out of unequal exchange.

Unequal exchange implies that as value is transferred from the periphery to the centre, the profit rate of the periphery falls but that of the latter rises. However, the over-exploitation of labour hinders the transition from absolute to relative surplus value as the dominant form in capital-labour relations, and also the process of accumulation in the dependent countries. The whole process further accentuates the problem of dependence.

Another important aspect of Marini's thesis relates to the *circuit of capital*. According to him, the circuit of capital in the centre and in the periphery are not the same. In the dominant countries, the phases of circulation of capital, namely, the production and the circulation, are completed and integrated internally (endogenously). Once the industrial capitalism has established itself in the advanced countries, capital accumulation will be based on increased relative surplus value of labour through the introduction of technical progress. As the labour productivity goes on increasing, capitalists can afford to allow wage boost without a fall in the rate of profit. Needless, to say, wage spurt leads to the desired increase in the effective demand for the capitalists' products (mainly industrial goods). And thus, the cycle continues and works smoothly.

However, in the dependent countries, things are different. In such countries, the two fundamental elements of the capital cycle (namely, production and the circulation of commodities) are separated as a result of periphery being linked to the centre through the over-exploitation of labour. In less developed countries, production does not rely on the internal capacity to consume but it depends on the exports to the developed countries. Marini observes that in periphery, workers are excluded from consuming manufactured goods. In fact, super-exploitation of workers means cheapening of the exported products, and cheaper reproduction of labour. Wages are kept low in dependent countries because the workers' consumption is not required for the realisation of commodities. Thus, conditions are created for the over-exploitation of labour so long as there exists a vast reserve of labour in the periphery.

The essential points of Marini's thesis can now be summed up:

Ruy Mauro Marini argues that underdevelopment persists in the periphery as the development of capitalism is constrained by the size of the capitalist market. In the LDCs, the worker's role is that of a producer and the product of its labour is exported. Since the product is exported, there is no need for the working class to save as consumers, and so its wages can be forced down. The workers are not required for the realisation in the dependent country. One implication of stagnant wage level is that market also remains stagnant and limited: market does not expand at all. The goods exported by the dependent countries are realised by the working class of the developed capitalist countries: the wage level is higher there. Marini argues that surplus value is produced in the periphery but it is appropriated in the centre. The surplus is transferred from the periphery to the centre through the mechanism of underconsumption of the working class.

Marini's analysis suffers from the following limitations. *First*, Marini does not consider the fact that super-exploitation of labour has a limit. Wages, in fact, cannot be reduced below the minimum subsistence level, for the workers would die of starvation, and this would be an obstacle for the expansion of capitalism. *Second*, contrary to Marini's belief, we find that workers' consumption (effective demand) does matter for production, income and employment. Before production, a producer has to reckon the demand for the product in the domestic market. *Lastly,* Marini's observation, that workers in the Third World countries do not consume manufactured goods, is not at all tenable. They do consume lots of manufactured items like clothes, food, medicines and the like. Marini states that the main reason responsible for the low wage in the less developed countries is the fact that workers' consumption is not required for the realisation of commodities. This is a mere obversion of truth. By virtue of their overwhelming numbers, workers do count in the domestic market in all types of developing countries. Low wages are the result of many socio-economic and institutional factors. However, all said, it must be conceded that Marini has been able to explain dependency in his own way through the introduction of some new analytical concepts which are at once original and thought-provoking.

(H) Gunnar Myrdal's Theory of Circular Causation

Gunnar Myrdal observes that in an underdeveloped economy, a process of circular causation is sure to start.[36] This process will have some effects which will be cumulative in the fashion that is similar to vicious circle idea. The forces will work in such a way that regional economic inequalities will be increased in an underdeveloped country. He contends that in the normal case, there is nothing in the social system as automatic self-stabilisation. The social system will generate forces which will not move towards any balance but will work to produce imbalance and inequality. He further remarks that usually nothing would work to counteract this inequality and therefore, the process will be cumulative and accelerated. In fact, circular causation provides a more rational explanation for the theoretical analysis of a social process than the stable equilibrium analysis. The principle of circular inter-dependence is valid in the field of entire social relations. Expansion in a locality produces two effects: (i) Backwash effects, and (ii) Spread effects. These are discussed below.

Backwash effects mean unfavourable effects. The backwash effects are generally produced through three factors – migration, capital and trade. These factors become favourable for a growing region but unfavourable for other regions. Economic expansion in a locality requires skill and efficient labourers who are brought from outside. Thus, the labourers become helpful for that growing community, where they are brought but the situation of the locality from which these labourers are brought, becomes unfavourable. In poorer localities again, fertility is higher and the diversion of population will lead to unfavourable age distribution. The situation in such localities may be worse when the relation between total population and resources would be unfavourable in the long-run. This was the case in Europe when rural people started migrating to industrial areas and to USA.

Similarly, capital movements will also increase regional inequalities. Capital will be shifted from a poor region to a prospering region where the rate of returns is high and capital is more secure. The demand for capital is higher in a progressive region because of the better opportunities for investment. Thus, progressive regions will draw more and more the savings of the poor regions. Hence, the poor regions will have increased inequality.

Trade is another factor which produces positive backwash effects on the growing regions and negative backwash effects on the stagnant poor regions. The progressive regions will have better competitive advantages and markets. The industries here will be having increasing returns and external economies which a poor region cannot enjoy. The poor regions will lack in the basic infrastructure. A poor region cannot afford to keep up a good communication system, and all other public utilities which are necessary for the expansion of trade will be inferior.

The poor regions will have low productive efficiency and will be highly tradition-bound. The entire social values in such a society will be against the experimental aspirations of a developing region. The circular causation will also act to sustain and expand these cumulative stagnating forces. Thus, a developing locality will produce some adverse effects, i.e., backwash effects, which will be reflected on other relatively poor localities, and thereby will increase inequalities. Backwash effects refer to the total cumulative effects that are caused by the process of circular causation between the economic and non-economic factors.

The growth of industrial localities can, however, also have some good effects for other areas. The whole region around a nodal centre of expansion will experience some advantageous effects as regards demand, technology, market, etc. These favourable effects, therefore, may be called the spread effects. As a result of expansion of certain localities, the nearby regions can supply agricultural raw materials and consumer goods and thereby can extend their market; while on the other hand, such regions can take the help of technical knowledge of the growing regions. Thus, the poor regions can also start new industries and can create new centres for economic expansion. But this is possible only when the retarding backwash effects are outweighed by the positive spread effects. The favourable spread effects become cumulative by circular causation and help to check the unfavourable influences of backwash effects.

But there is, however, no reason to assume that backwash and spread effects will be in equilibrium. In rare cases, the two effects may be in equilibrium, which will mean a situation of stagnation. This equilibrium will be unstable, because any change in the forces will move it upward or downward. There are reasons to believe that backwash effects will be predominant in an underdeveloped country. In underdeveloped economies, the historical pattern of growth suggests that the spread effects are generally weak. In many cases, it is evident that the growth of the industrial sector did not much expand the market of cash crops of the rural sector; nor did the agricultural sector produce raw materials for the industrial sector. Economic Commission for Europe reports two important correlations: (i) regional disparities are greater in poor countries than the rich ones, and (ii) the disparities are decreasing in rich countries but are increasing in poor countries. Myrdal contends that these correlations may be explained by the fact that the higher the magnitude of economic development, the higher would be spread effects.

If backwash effects are neutralised, a spur for development will be created which will sustain the tempo almost automatically, provided the spread effects are very strong. In other words, a low level of economic development with weak spread effects will create, by circular causation, more inequalities, which will hold back economic progress. On the other hand, a higher level of development will strengthen the spread effects and will thereby minimise inequalities which may be more helpful for economic development. There may be so many other counteracting changes which will tend to retard progress; for instance, external diseconomies, increasing private and public expenditures, high wages, etc. But Myrdal believes that these checks cannot retard an economy below a certain level. If these retarding forces are permanent, a low level stable equilibrium will be established. However, changes of anticipation following a more primary change may push up a cumulative process in the same direction. A social process will entail a great variety of differently interconnected changes in response to a primary change. These changes may counteract but broadly they will support each other. "....A boom will probably always increase the relative strength of the spread effects. A depression will decrease it...".

Myrdal uses the concept of backwash effects in the realm of international trade also. He observes that the trade between advanced and underdeveloped countries is really increasing the discrepancy between the level of productivity in those countries. International trade is producing strong backwash effects on underdeveloped countries which are evident in the pattern of production of these countries. Myrdal says that instead of producing primary goods for export, the underdeveloped countries should better improve the productivity of the primary sector, and develop manufactures. In the absence of exchange control, it is possible that capital would flow out of backward countries. International adjustment through migration is not possible in such countries at the present moment.

The colonial policies held back progress and led to stagnation or regression. The heritage cannot be dispelled by mere political freedom, because such policies created strong cumulative social process and strengthened unfavourable circular causation. This is true in the case of Asian and African countries. Therefore, Myrdal advocates the necessity of a new theory of international trade for the underdeveloped countries.

With the help of backwash and spread effects, Myrdal successfully analyses how the poorer regions remain mainly agricultural with low level of productivity and how they cannot succeed easily in accelerating the process of industrialisation. The ideas of backwash and spread effects are, however, not his own. Hla Myint has already given similar explanations. The basic idea of Myrdal resembles Harrod's theory of cumulative movements away from equilibrium. Myrdal carries the arguments further than Myint and his concept is at the same time broader than Harrod's, for it includes social as well as economic aspects of equilibrium.

(I) Anthony Giddens's Evolutionary Theory of Development and Change

At the outset, it must be borne in mind that although Giddens does not explicitly describe any theory of evolution as such, a careful reader can get some idea about evolution and historical stages in his work. This is evident in his analysis of different types of societies.[37] It is now necessary to understand the formal distinction between social integration and system integration. Whereas social integration refers to face-to-face direct reciprocity between actors, system integration implies reciprocity between groups or collective bodies. In his classificatory schema, there are basically three types of societies. Tribal societies are largely based on direct face-to-face integration. In such societies, social integration and system integration imply the same thing. But in the second type of class-divided societies, social integration and system integration become different, although the level of integration is comparatively low. There may be a symbiotic relation between the rural and the urban areas. Social classes exist in class-divided societies but the class system is not central. In a class society, there is a separation of social and system integration at the high level, and the division between rural and urban areas becomes meaningless because these exist in created environment: the urban sector becomes more important.

According to Giddens, different types of societies exist alongside each other and there is no inevitable progression from one to the other. However, he is much concerned with the transition to industrial society i.e. from class-divided to class-dominated societies. His classification of societies smacks of a loose evolutionary theory; the transition from a tribal society to an industrial society is after all a matter of evolution.

In Giddens's analysis, a system has its own laws of development, however weak.[38] Implicit in his writing is the idea that every social system has its own phenomenology and uniqueness from other systems. The systemic differences are rooted through the process of *disembedding* which involves emptying of time and space. The analysis of the development of modernity gives an impression that it is historically inevitable. The inevitability of modernity is also explained by *reflexivity*. In a given social system, say, modern world, it becomes necessary to find rational explanation of every phenomenon; dependence on tradition or faith is not justified in any way.

128

In Giddens's analysis, modernity is understood as industrialism.[39] In his view, industrialism refers social relations implied in the widespread use of material power and machinery in the process of production. In the real world of modernity, we always try to *reembed* our relationships. Giddens considers post modernism as the product and the last stage of modernism.

Capitalism is another important dimension of modernity. He defines capitalism as a system of commodity production involving both competitive product market and the commodification of labour power. Capitalism is one of the main institutional dimensions of modernity and the process of capital accumulation represents one of the driving forces of modern institutions. Modernity institutionalises doubt or suspicion everywhere. Thus, search for more knowledge, information and expertise becomes extremely essential through a good deal of reskilling. In the situation of uncertainty and multi choice generated by modernity, trust gives a sense of ontological security and becomes a medium of interaction with the abstract systems which both empty the traditional notion from daily existence and set up congenial atmosphere for globalising influences. The more tradition loses its hold and the more is the importance of the dialectical interplay of the local and global forces, the more diversified becomes the choice of life style.

Modernity produces differences, exclusions and marginalisation: inequalities and class differentiation are cases in point. Modernity is essentially a post-order system and in such a situation, transformation of time and space coupled with disembedding mechanisms take the social life away from the clutches of traditional order. Here lies the importance of reflexivity which is the third major influence on the dynamism of modern institutions. The offshoots of modernity such as reorganisation of time and space, disembedding mechanisms and reflexivity presume universalising properties that can explain the tendency towards expansion and change. The change may reach the global dimension.

Globalisation is a dialectical phenomenon in which events at one extreme may produce divergent or contrary events at another. In such a system , none can stay away from the transformation brought about by modernity. The processes of change engendered by modernity are connected to the influences of globalisation. Modernity is beset with various types of risk which can be quantified and evaluated in order to make proper choice. According to Giddens, in modern social conditions, crises become more or less endemic. At many levels, modernity is just prone to crisis. A crisis may occur whenever activities concerned with goals suddenly become inadequate. The crisis-prone nature of modernity has unsettling consequences at least for two reasons. First, it leads to create or intensify the climate of uncertainty, and second, it exposes everyone to the diversity of crisis. In conditions of high modernity, however, crisis becomes normalised. Giddens's view of crisis is similar to Marx's. Marx thought that periodic crisis is a normal feature of capitalism.

Modernity ushers in an era of war and conflict. This view of Giddens can be applied to the analysis of dependency or interdependence brought about by modernity. It can be said that the developing economies cannot really escape from the pervasive system of globalisation, but there would be many areas of conflict between DCs and LDCs and that the latter group of countries will be possibly exploited by the former. The inequalities between them would be widening in the higher stage of modernity i.e. globalism. All this is implied by the theory developed by Giddens on modernity. Giddens's structuration theory is a postmodernist theory that discusses, among others, the development of neo-functionalism and symbolic interaction.[40] One of the ideas developed in this great book is that in the post-modern period, societies and institutions have developed in such a way that they are beyond the power of human control.

Be that as it may, Giddens's analysis is not free from criticism. Giddens is a critique of any sort of evolutionary theory but his own analysis of different types of society, and the implicit transformation from one type into another, gives one the idea that although different types of societies may exist side by side, the modern urban society was basically a traditional society to begin with and it has been transformed into the modern society. The evolutionary perspective cannot altogether be brushed aside.

It is indeed problematic to precisely define *social system* after Giddens. Giddens says social systems are defined by the clusterings of institutions. The definition is operationally imprecise especially for the purpose of comparison over time and over geographical areas. Equally disquieting is his assertion that unintended consequences can be an explanation for the existence of ordered social system.

Ian Craib rightly says that if order were an unintended consequence of action, we should also expect chaos to be an unintended consequence as well. But action theory cannot offer a valid explanation of why we do not get chaos. Giddens makes a great deal of the notions of time and space at two different levels: one, the phenomenology of time and space, and the other, as methodology of analysing social systems. Unless these uses are clearly separated, there may be confusion for the readers to comprehend the real issues.[41]

Notes

1.   Celso Furtado, *Development and Underdevelopment*, University of California Press, California, 1964, p. 141.
2.   Ibid, p.142.
3.   Ibid., p. 143. He has given a number of historical examples to bring home this point.
4.   Celso Furtado, "The Concept of External Dependence in the Study of Underdevelopment", in Charles K. Wilber (ed.) *Political Economy of Development and Underdevelopment*, Random House, New York, 1973, p. 118.
5.   Ibid., p. 120.
6.   Ibid., p. 122.
7.   Geoffrey Kay, *Development and Underdevelopment*, Macmillan, London, 1975.
8.   Ibid., p. 103.
9.   Ibid., p. 100.
10.   Ibid., Preface, p. (x).
11.   F. H. Cardoso, "Dependency and Development in Latin America", *New Left Review*, July-August, 1972; and F. H. Cardoso and E. Faletto, *Dependency and Development in Latin America*, University of California Press, USA, 1979.
12.   Bill Warren, "Imperialism and Capitalist Industrialisation", *New Left Review*, Sept., 1973.
13.   Bill Warren, *Imperialism: The Pioneer of Capitalism*, Verso, 1982, p. 162.
14.   H. Gulalp, "Debate on Capitalism and Development", *Capital and Class*, Spring 1986, p. 149.
15.   Bill Warren, *Imperialism: The Pioneer of Capitalism, Op. Cit.*, p. 129. Warren's idea is influenced by Marx's earlier assertion that British capital did many good things for India.
16.   As quoted in Oxaal et al. (eds.), *Beyond the Sociology of Development: Economy and Society in Latin America and Africa*, Routledge and Kegan Paul, London, 1975, p. 5.
17.   Osvaldo Sunkel, "National Development Policy and External Dependency in Latin America", *Journal of Development Studies*, Oct. 1989, p. 28.
18.   *Loc. Cit.*
19.   Osvaldo Sunkel, *Op. Cit.*, p. 33.
20.   Osvaldo Sunkel, "Transnational Capitalism and National Integration", *Social and Economic Studies*, Special Number, March 1973.
21.   I.M. Wallerstein, *The Modern World System*, Academic Press, New York, 1974, p. 229.
22.   Ibid., p. 230.
23.   Ibid., p. 231.
24.   Ibid., p. 235.
25.   A. P. Appleby, "Review: The Modern World System", *The American Historical Review*, Vol. 80, 1975, p. 1323.

26. Stuart Corbridge, *Capitalist World Development*, Macmillan, London, 1956 p.34.
27. Ibid., p. 35.
28. H. Gulalp, "Frank and Wallerstein Revisited", in P. Limqueco and Bruce McFarlane (eds.), *Neo-Marxist Theories of Development*, Croom Helm, Kent, 1983, p. 125.
29. Ibid., p. 129.
30. Ibid., p. 131.
31. J. N. Pieterse, "A Critique of World System Theory", *Kajian Malaysia*, December 1987, p. 4.
32. F. Braudel, *The Perspective of the World Civilization and Capitalism*, Harper & Row, 1961.
33. A.B. Appleby, *Op. Cit.*, p. 1324.
34. R. M. Marini, *Dialectica de la Dependencia*, Ediciones Era, Mexico, 1973.
35. Cristobal Kay, "Reflections on the Latin American Contribution to Development Theory", *Development and Change*, January, 1991, p. 50.
36. Gunnar Myrdal (1958), *Economic Theory and Underdeveloped Regions*, Macmillan, p. 28 ff.
37. Ian Craib, *Modern Social Theory*, Harvester Wheatsheaf, UK 1992, p. 118.
38. Anthony Giddens (1990), *The Consequences of Modernity*, Polity Press, Oxford, 1990.
39. Anthony Giddens, (1992) *Modernity and Self-Identity*, Polity Press, Cambridge, p. 15.
40. G. A. Bryant and D. Jary (eds.) (1991), *Giddens' Theory of Structuration*, Routledge, London.
41. Ian Craib, (1992), *Anthony Giddens*, Routledge, London.

9 Contemporary Issues in the Dependency Debate

One of the serious misconceptions in the theory of development and underdevelopment is the belief that dependency theory is dead forever and that it has no relevance in the modern world. However, contrary to the general belief, it must be conceded that the dependency debate is not really over as yet. It is indeed a very relevant explanation for the growing economic distance between developed and developing countries and also for the slow growth of the latter countries.

There are indeed many issues and areas of development where dependency plays a major role. Some of these are: aid dependency, technological dependency, dependency for foreign capital investment, trade dependency, dependency for better human capital formation and so forth. In all these areas, developing countries are made to depend on the developed countries (DCs) which take full advantage of the situation in exploiting the poor countries.

Dependency involves considerable *moral hazard* which works to jeopardise the process of development of less developed countries (LDCs). For instance, dependency on the IMF for financial resources distorts developing countries' incentive to develop their own financial resources. On the other hand, such a dependency does give full power in the hands of the IMF to play ducks and drakes with the socioeconomic life of the dependent country. Thus, as the financial crisis of the East Asian economies at the beginning of this country reveals, the IMF advice, even if it is wrong, is accepted without opposition and protest by many affected countries.

In the name of helping the poor countries, the developed countries have been constantly trying to extract surplus from them through so-called foreign aid, unequal trade, technology transfer and the like. The exploitation continues unabated even today but through subtler mechanism and mode. In the nineteenth century, the metropolitan DCs used to take away the physical capital from colonies by force after annexing them. However, since the twentieth century, particularly after the independence of some colonies in the Third World, erstwhile colonial powers had to change their *modus operandi* of extracting capital from these countries. Whereas earlier it was physical capital, later on human capital extraction has become the main target of DCs without paying any compensation to the brain-sending developing countries (see Ghosh, 1999). The phenomenon is commonly known as brain drain.

Globalisation is another capitalist mechanism to entangle the LDCs in the sophisticated world capitalist framework to subject them to compete in the unequal competitive regime and to make them more dependent on the DCs. Globalisation is not a new phenomenon; it was present in the nineteenth century and worked in favour of the imperialist powers.

In the present chapter, an attempt will be made to briefly analyse some of the current issues in the dependency debate. These issues include world monetary system and the new international economic disorder, technological imperialism, the issue of human development and human rights and so on.

(i) Dependency and Development: Intertemporal Paradigm Shifts

Although the relation between dependency and development/ under development was recognised in the fifties of the last century, the nexus was not formerly brought to bear immediately in the analysis of the problem of underdevelopment. Development economics (DE) recognised the inter-relations rather late through intertemporal paradigm shifts. The present section briefly discusses the paradigm shifts in DE to appreciate the way and the time of recognition of the importance of the problem of dependency in the analysis of development and underdevelopment.

Ever since its inception as a new subject, DE has been pursuing its basic desideratum of amelioration of poverty, increase in employment and income, elimination of diseases, malnutrition and undernutrition from the world, especially from the Third World, by means of growth and development. It is in this sense that one can say that there is a continuity of purpose and action sustained by DE over the last fifty years. However, in spite of purposive unicity and continuity, DE has been experiencing new challenges and constraints, and the response to these issues and problems has induced paradigm shifts in the subject.

The 1950s can be described as a decade of *theoretical innovations* in DE. Many theories of development that were put forward during this period attempted to explain the existence of underdevelopment from various perceptual angles, and accordingly suggested remedies to the problem of backwardness and poverty. The approach was simplistic and non-technical, easily comprehensible by planners and policy-makers. The attainment of economic growth was the fundamental objective set for the Third World countries, for it was presumed that economic growth could automatically solve the problems of poverty, unemployment and other associated problems, and immediate attention was not paid to the dependency relation that caused the debacle.

The 1960s are often regarded as the *golden period* and a decade of optimism in development economics.[1] Development was more objectively defined as a blend of growth and change. While new theories of growth and development were forthcoming, some of the old theories and issues were refined and reconciled. Influenced by the Keynesian economic theory, positive role was assigned to the state to manage economic growth and development. It was thought that foreign aid and technical assistance from DCs would be able to make a dent in poverty and unemployment. Many Third World countries initiated economic planning with gusto and grist but the outcome was not commensurate with the efforts. It was soon realised that despite concerted efforts for a decade, and the realisation of around 5 per cent economic growth by LDCs, the basic problem of poverty and inequality in these countries could not be perceptibly reduced. And on the other hand, the economic gap between DCs and LDCs was widening due to uneven development of the centre and the periphery. The periphery started losing resources for paying high interests on borrowed capital from the centre. The optimism with which the decade started off could not be sustained, and a sense of pessimism entered the arena of DE.

The 1970s can be looked upon as a *decade of reappraisal*. The achievement of 5 per cent rate of growth was not sustainable, and poverty and inequality intensified in most of the poor countries. Economic growth as the basic desideratum of DE was challenged by many economists, and it was thought that blind application of western growth models was not only inappropriate but also harmful, for these caused enormous mal-development to LDCs. For the first time, it was realised that the dependency model of development was the cause of socioeconomic retrogression. All these called for *limits to growth*.

On the other end of the spectrum, one could discern growing economic domination by DCs through trade and aid. The debt burden of LDCs started increasing, and it was realised that trade was not the engine of growth;

rather, it was a mechanism immiserising growth. The negative externalities of large industrial projects in terms of ecological costs looked conspicuously overwhelming. The New International Economic Order reflected these issues for the first time.

Basic human needs including education, health and employment and the like were regarded as the correct components of development which were reflected in the formulation of *basic needs approach* to development popularised by the World Bank and UN Research Institute for Social Development. The agenda for employment generation was the main agenda in this development decade. The most significant achievement of this development decade was the realisation that it was distribution rather than production *per se* which was necessary for ensuring basic needs required for human development, and the capitalist rule of production-centric materialist game would not take the economy to the desired goal.

The 1980s are characterised as a *lost decade* in development economics for many obvious reasons of which the following remain important: first, in the course of time, many contradictions became evident in simplistic economistic paradigm of development.[2] Development became unstable and volatile in many countries[3] and there was apparent failure of conventional theories of development.

Second, the welfare state of the Keynesian type did not bring any longer any hope for solving the problems relating to underdevelopment and poverty; and at other end of the continuum, there was a smouldering discontent both against capitalism and socialism for their failure to show a viable road to growth and development in poor countries. Third, while the countries in the South were trying to find out alternative driving forces for socioeconomic changes in the desired direction, they constantly castigated the North as responsible for their sad plight: the North-South debate became more vociferous and vitriolic. Fourth, the new international economic order lost its momentum, and could be dubbed as a system of new international economic disorder. Contrary to the expectation of people, less capital and less technology flowed to the LDCs from DCs; and there was also *reverse transfer of technology* in the form of *brain drain* from the poor to the rich countries.[4] Fifth, there was an apparent disillusionment with aid and trade as mechanisms for helping the desired process of development. Both trade and aid became means for *surplus extraction* from the poor countries. The temper of time suggested alternative strategies for people's empowerment, participation and grass root development with top down planning process, settlement of gender conflict, elimination of, or at least, reduction in ecological imbalance, and a powerful civil society that can bring about social changes. The theory of dependency was highly acclaimed as the most appropriate theory for the explanation of slow relative growth and poverty in LDCs.

Thus, there were indeed many types of debates, conflicts, issues and questions during the decade. But there was no synthesis and solutions in the offing, and neither was there any new consensus on the feasible strategic action and direction. In the words of W. A. Lewis, the development economics was in complete doldrums.

The 1990s will go down in the annals of DE as the decade of *new vision and new direction*. The decade has witnessed attempts for re-development after years of mal-developments in the Third World countries. The entire development process so far based on state planning and patronage came in for serious criticism, and more reliance was placed in market as an organising mechanism for global relations.[5] Privatisation which was already in the agenda in many developing countries occupied the front seat in terms of priority. But towards the end of the decade, the limitations of free market mechanism came to the surface with the financial crisis of the East Asian economies. Perhaps, it was a new perception. Economic underpinnings of the development paradigms came once again under critical scrutiny with feminist movement taking the lead.[6] Instigated by the Beijing conference of 1995, the whole gamut of issues concerning gender was recast, and the earlier notion of *women in development* was replaced by the more comprehensive issue of *gender and development*.

There has been mounting pressure from the Third World to reform the UN, to democratise the WTO, and to make the international institutions more accountable and transparent in their dealings. It was realized that the old institutions like IMF and World Bank need structural changes to effectively deal with the financial crisis of the Asian countries. The civil society movement which was prominent in the early 1990s became very positive and innovative in its agenda for action asking for all-round policy changes both within and without. Globalisation was the most publicised and confused slogan in this decade. It reminds one of the exploitative globalisation of the nineteenth country, and many well-informed groups have been trying to spin away from it because the MNC-led globalisation may unleash a regime of unequal competition between DCs and LDCs, and this may be destructive to economic and social development processes. These groups are engaged in achieving self-sufficiency and autonomy while recognising limits to competition in the globalised world. The focus, however, shifted from the question of underdevelopment to the problem caused by industrial development. Human and social dimensions of development which were emphasised in international conferences from 1992 to 1996 are going to get upper hand, and are likely to be the basic theme song of DE in the new millennium.

(ii) Human Development and Human Rights

Development does not necessarily mean that one should have more but that one should be more. Thus, development essentially entails human development. It is contrary to the capitalist concept of development which is measured in terms of the rate of growth of GNP or material production. Disillusionment with the western concept of development came to focus in the seventies of the last century, and the concept of human development came to the forefront. The basic needs approach was introduced as a more suitable measure of development. The basic needs included both physical and cultural needs. The basic needs approach can be regarded as social indicators of development and rests on human development approach. Initially, the following six basic needs were considered, e.g. nutrition, basic education, health sanitation, water supply, housing and related infrastructure.[7]

Human development as an indicator of economic development is not used in the dependency type of development model for many obvious reasons. First, human development (HD) does not indicate material progress as is emphasised in the capitalist dependency model. Second, it goes against the production-centric western notion of development. Third, the political economy of dependency suggests that domination over better educated and informed people is rather difficult than that over poor, uneducated and ignorant people. However, the UNDP started the exercise of formulation of human development index (HDI) to gauge the comparative development of different countries and to appreciate the tempo of socioeconomic development of a country since 1990. The classic study by Morris (1979) for measuring the physical quality of life index (PQLI) was an important addition to measure human development.[8] A. K. Sen argued that development essentially means the substantive freedom to achieve the capabilities of human beings. And the construction of HDI reflects an attempt to capture basic capabilities of human beings. Since relative inequalities in human development may induce absolute capability

138

failures, the UNDP started disaggregated country studies by race, religion and other categories.[9] However, surprisingly, there was no freedom index in the early studies of the UNDP.

The measurement of human development which is a pro-people concept has been constrained by many factors. First, adjusted income taken as a proxy of welfare leaves scopes for criticisms. Second, the indicators cannot be made universal. But these should be specific and contextual and, third, the same indicators cannot be used for both DCs and LDCs. Thus, distinct approaches are necessary to make the measurement fool-proof. But there are indeed many conceptual and methodological problems. For instance, it is pretty difficult to compare the acquisition of knowledge by people of different countries as also the true components of knowledge.

Be that as it may, HDI is a significant step forward in the computation of development or progress in recent years. The most important dimension in this regard is the treatment of ethical issues relating to poverty, deprivation, empowerment and entitlement.[10] HDI, however, cannot explain many interrelations among agents, principles and their relations, and it cannot also explain many socioeconomic, institutional and political forces that ride the crest of the globalisation process of the modern world. Human development which incorporates ethical issues should focus on the normative and positive nature of interactions in the grassroot planning process. The Human Development Report (1998) has pointed out that while the fortunate rich countries have gained from globalisation in terms of increasing consumption, the poor people have gained only marginally. "….The poorest 20 per cent of the world's people and more have been left out of the consumption explosion. Well over a billion people are deprived of basic consumption needs. Of the 4.4 billion people in developing countries, nearly three-fifths lack basic sanitation. Almost a third have no access to clean water. A quarter does not have adequate housing. A fifth have no access to modern health services. A fifth of children do not attend school to grade 5, and so on in the list of deprivation…".

In the situation of uncertainty and moral hazard that dependency generates, human development and basic human rights cannot be ensured through empowerment and entitlement. The issue of human rights without the guarantee of basic human needs and development becomes an empty issue indeed. A Conference in Vienna (1999) on human rights ended in a fiasco. All was over with only *Pussy Cat Syndrome*: nothing substantial could be achieved indeed. The failure of the conference mainly stems from its inability to take stock of the global political economy vis-à-vis human rights problems. If one looks at the global scenario, one will encounter situations which cannot be said to be congenial to human rights. In fact, these situations will imply negation of human rights, particularly for the South. Let us have a close look at the global scenario.

The UN Security Council has had a peculiar mechanism of ultimate decision-making. The veto power can be exercised by five members. Only one member is selected from the Third World countries, although these countries represent 75 per cent of the world population. Moreover, the opinion of this member does not convey any effective weightage. The decision-making group is dominated by the USA, the Uncle Sam of global political economy. The UN Security Council is so dominated by the USA that it has virtually become a US Security Council.

The domination of the UN by the USA is evident in several instances like the case of Libya, sanctions against Iraq immediately after the Gulf War, and bombardment on Iraq by the USA after the war and so forth, almost *ad infinitum*. Even the General Assembly is not free from US hegemony, for the democratic process is not fully followed there and the members are often intimidated, bullied and even blackmailed. The UN is no longer a global democratic organisation. It is out and out a pro-US institution.

With the virtual demise of the Soviet countervailing system, the world is now left with a single super-power, the USA. The end of the Gulf War was the real beginning of US hegemony not only over the Gulf region but also over the entire developing nations. Through willy nilly skullduggery, the USA went against the UN sanction by attacking the civilians of Iraq, bombing schools, hospitals and religious places. In the modern system of unipolar global political economy, the people of the Third World cannot even fully follow their internal political-economic policy without being dependent on the US system.

Global political economy is based on an unfair and unjust system. The so-called world organisations like the IMF, World Bank, GATT and the like are dominated by the group of Big Seven. The interests of the South are always conveniently neglected. The global system is unequal in many respects. For instance, between 1960 and 1990, the countries with the richest 20 per cent of world population increased their share of global wealth from 70 per cent to 83 per cent whereas for the countries with the poorest 20 per cent of the world population, the share of global wealth fell from 2.3 per cent to 1.5 per cent. In 1960, the top 20 per cent of the world's countries received income 30 times more than that of bottom 20 per cent level countries. Moreover by 1990, the share of the top 20 per cent went up 60 times. The disparities in the consumption levels are even more disquieting. The developed countries, with about 25 per cent of the world population, consume about 70 per cent of the world's energy, 75 per cent of its metal, 85 per cent of its wood and 60 per cent of its food resources.

The contrasting picture in less developed countries (LDCs) is highly mortifying: about one billion adults are illiterate, one billion live below the poverty line and one and a half billion people are deprived of primary health-care facilities. Life is indeed nasty, brutish and short. A large proportion of LDCs do not enjoy even the minimum amount of basic economic, political and social human rights. Moreover, about 100 million people live below the poverty line in the developed market economies.

The LDCs are highly indebted countries. Their indebtedness to the IMF went up from $10 billion to $49 billion in 1960, and mounting debt servicing charges often eat away a good bit of their budgetary resources. The LDCs are not only poor and indebted but they are also dependent in many ways on the DCs for so-called aid, trade, investment, technology transfer and so on. Owing to the peculiar dependency nexus in the global political economy, the present-day LDCs possess hopelessly unequal and weaker bargaining power.

Apparently, the North seems to have a deeply condescending view, often termed as Eurocentrism, *Weltanschauung,* towards the Third World. But the western concept of human rights is erroneously synonymous with political and civil rights. A large number of people in the Third World are seen to simply exist amidst poverty and destitution, and not living with human dignity. The DCs consider themselves the vectors of human salvation, do not bother about the violation of economic rights. Their policy to link aid with human rights is designed mainly to curb the economic progress of LDCs. In fact, if the violation of economic rights is regarded as a violation of basic human rights, the DCs stand equally guilty too.

Be that as it may, unless the inequalities between the North and South are completely eliminated, the talk about human rights will be mere "....idle bubble blowing....". When the present global political economy is full of cooperative conflicts, and a sizable proportion of mankind stand less human and less equal, none but rational fools are likely to be carried away by the shibboleth of human rights.

(iii) Technological Imperialism

Technology is the technical knowledge which is used in production or embodied in capital or machinery. Technology transfer implies the transfer of technical knowledge from one country to another either through a deliberate government policy or by private channels of communications. The agencies involved in the transfer of technology are government, commercial enterprises such as multinational corporations (MNCs), private agencies or international non-profit organisations.

Technology supplied by developed countries to the less developed countries (LDCs) is either too sophisticated for LDCs to adapt or too obsolete to reduce the cost of production. Most of the technology transferred to the LDCS is, therefore, not appropriate. LDCs may be more harmed than helped by inappropriate products as well as inappropriate techniques because, such techniques and products are not consistent with the requirements, standards and income levels of these countries. LDCs had better develop their own technology and products suitable for their own circumstances. Imported large-scale capital-intensive technology is not necessarily better than indigenous small-scale labour-intensive technology. Advanced technology may reduce both real income and employment in the LDCs. The imported technology may be not only inappropriate but may also kill the initiative and innovative enterprise. The local conditions may be such that foreign technology may not be productively absorbed.

In the LDCs, the people are tradition-bound and do not generally favour the introduction of sophisticated technology, which is not only costly but also requires skilled and technical personnel for its application. LDCs are proverbially capital-shy and the level of human capital formation is also low in such countries. However, western juggernaut technology is not necessary, strictly speaking, in LDCs. Since factor endowments are different in different countries, the same kind of technology may not be useful everywhere. Technology transfer is very likely to bring in its wake technological domination by and dependence on the foreign countries.

The MNCs not only ask for a high price for the transfer of technology but also want to keep control over it so that the competitors are not able to know the secrets. Sometimes the Governments of the LDCs are under the false impression that only imported technology furthers the cause of national development. Often, it is not realised that the development of the strategic sectors or industries by imported technology may be dangerous in the long-run. Evidently, technology transfer has increased inequalities in

LDCs. Also, it is not efficient. In case, technology is imported into LDCs, it needs to be regulated and assimilated to suit the local needs.

Concentrated control of technology is one of the most effective means of establishing oligopoly power in LDCs and of restricting the development of local competition. The foreign technology is highly capital-intensive and does not suit the conditions of LDCs where capital is scarce and labour is in plenty. In the MNCs drug companies in India, labour cost comes to only 5 per cent of the total cost. The capital intensity is so high that it costs $50,000 to provide one job. Robert McNamara once gave an example. A modern plastic shoe factory costing $100,000, he said, employed only 40 persons and rendered 50,000 traditional shoe-makers and their suppliers jobless. The technology of MNCs destroys far more jobs than it creates. This kind of contradiction in MNCs sponsored capitalist development is inherent. The export-processing enclave being developed by MNCs in some countries is integrated with the MNCs' production system which is capitalist in nature and is not integrated with the rest of the economy. It develops a dualistic structure which cannot compromise with the process of development the LDCs are pursuing. Almost all technology in LDCs comes from and is controlled by MNCs.

The MNCs only diffuse and do not transfer technology. They are also reluctant to take up technology adaptation programmes. UNCTAD has calculated that LDCs spend $17,000 to $18,000 million per year for the purchase of western technology. If this amount is spent on R&D programmes, the LDCs can well hope to attain technological self-reliance. The technology that is transferred by the MNCs to the subsidiaries is secondhand but comes at a higher price than that in the open market. In the case of Mexico, the managers admitted that over-valuation of their technology is a common factor. In some cases, such overpricing comes to 300 to 680 per cent. In spite of high price of transfer, the secret of production is not given out to the buyer. For instance, the Coco-Cola company did not part with the formula of the drink. When the technology becomes obsolete and unprofitable in the home country, it is transferred to LDCs. But even in that case the transfer takes place with many restrictions regarding production, sales and exports. LDCs cannot properly assimilate foreign technology and their absorption capacity is also probably low.

Surprisingly enough, the same technology is sold to many firms in the same country and, sometimes, technology is sold to LDCs only for a part of the production process. In this way, the dependency of LDCs is very carefully maintained by the peddlers of foreign technology. This implies that for competing goods, indigenous production has to depend on MNCs. In fact, in the name of technology transfer, MNCs are suppressing the potentially prospective sector which can otherwise become the source of development.

While LDCs want to do away with backwardness and dependence by importing technology from the west, the west instead transfers technology in such a way that the dependence is not only sustained but is gradually increased. Technology transfer is a means of integrating LDCs with the capitalist of process growth. Technology purchase is a huge burden. UNCTAD has estimated that direct payment for technology bought by LDCs accounted to $1,500 million in 1968 and more than $20,000 million in 1980. India paid $4,000 to foreign technicians in 1960 – 61. This amount rose to paid $66 million in 1969-70. For the LDCs, the cost of technology import is expected to go up to $100-150 billion by the year 2000.

The MNCs create a demand for their products in LDCs through a transfer of tastes. The present system of technology import through MNCs tends to perpetuate technological dependence. In fact, transfer of inappropriate technology has, instead of narrowing the chasm, considerably increased the international inequalities and dependence.

To take the case of India, despite 4,000 collaborations approved since 1948 in India, the technology gap is still wide and has been widening. Much of India's technology is outdated, repetitive and the cause of low productivity. Parliament's Committee on Public Undertakings found that the public sector undertakings in India have been indiscriminatingly entering into foreign technical collaborations in spite of the fact that the required technology is available in the country itself. The 89th Report (5th Lok Sabha) points out that there are several instances of foreign collaborations by private parties when the technology was available with the local public undertakings in India. One such instance is the collaboration for the production of nitroleloume by a Bombay firm though Hindustan Organic Chemicals (Pune) already had the know how, Indian Oxygen Limited had entered into foreign collaborations for an oxygen plant when Bharat Heavy Plant and Vessels (Vishakhpatnam) had the necessary know-how. Texmaco (Calcutta) went in for foreign collaboration for industrial boilers when BHEL (Trichy) had the necessary know-how. There are many more such instances. In some cases, India can introduce her own goods with her own technology but still she borrows foreign technology,

India's technology policy, like that of many other LDCs, is neither firm nor consistent, and seems to be influenced by political considerations.

Basically, the policy is to have selective import of technology. Technology is imported when there is a delay in the development of indigenous technology and a particular target cannot be achieved. It took 20 years to build up the Bokaro Steel Plant because reliance was placed on foreign technology. The policy indicates appropriate measures to facilitate technology diffusion, including horizontal transfer. In this direction, a collaborative arrangement is simply not enough. Regarding import, the decision is taken by businessmen and bureaucrats, and not by technologists. This is something strange. There is, therefore, multiple and repetitive import of the same or similar technology under different collaboration agreements.

Most of the technology that LDCs import is not useful for the production of mass consumption goods, especially for use by those who live below the poverty line. The argument based alone on the efficiency criterion for the import of technology is to obfuscate the vital issues. The decision to import should be left with the scientific community rather than with the bureaucrats. What is ultimately at stake is the quality of the growth process, the goals and objectives of the growth itself. It is an issue of slow growth with self-reliance versus a bit higher growth with dependency. However, it appears that technological dependency is there to stay on for a long time in LDCs.

(iv) Brain Drain and Reverse Transfer of Technology

Brain drain representing the outflow of underutilised or overutilised skilled manpower from the low developed countries (LDCs)to developed countries (DCs) en masse on a regular scale, has received considerable amount of importance in the literature on economic development of the Third World countries.[11] The problem of brain drain has been made a part of the explanation of economic backwardness and *reverse transfer of technology.* Needless to say, the backwardness of the developing countries is the main cause of brain drain, and conversely, it is the brain drain itself which contributes to curbing the development process of these countries. This is so because the outflow of high quality manpower (HQM) constitutes a loss to the sending-country in the sense that although such manpower is vitally important in the drama of development of LDCs, it is wooed away by the deliberate neocolonialist policy of the DCs. The losses involved in brain drain have several socioeconomic dimensions.[12] It is an empirical truth that

145

a country following a colonial development policy generates a higher magnitude of brain drain than what is otherwise possible.

The present section seeks to argue that the problem of brain drain is generated and intensified by the deliberate neo-imperialistic policy of developed capitalist countries which are still exploiting the LDCs under the new garb of so-called foreign aid and development assistance programmes. In fact, brain drain can be viewed as a problem of *reverse flow of technology* from the LDCs to the DCs rather than the other way round. The exploitation continues unabated but in a different fashion in the sense that, while in the pre-industrial revolution, the capitalist countries drew resources from the colonies in the form of physical capital, in the post-industrial revolution period, they are drawing away the human capital resources from the LDCs. The motive and the effect in both the cases remain more or less the same with only little nuances.

Brain drain is a one-way permanent migration of productively employed HQM mostly from LDCs to DCs. Needless to say, the outflow of this strategic manpower creates many structural mal-adjustments and produces enormous negative externalities and thereby retards the process of economic development of the brain-losing country. The gain derived from the brain overflow is more than offset by the loss sustained due to brain drain. The advantages of the phenomenon of brain overflow have often been overplayed by the writers of capitalist countries. As a matter of fact, brain overflow often involves uneducated and semi-educated manpower which is not permitted to inflow by the immigration laws of developed countries (DCs). Thus, the importance of brain overflow as the source of supply of valuable forex in LDCs is gradually declining. But on the other hand, the gravity of the problem of brain drain for LDCs is gradually increasing as these countries have limited stocks of physical capital, HQM and narrow technology frontier.

The most important item in the international intercourse today is not food, fuel or fibre, but transaction in technology. The USA every year exports technology to the extent of $9,000 million but imports only $1,000 million worth of technology. To correct her structural imbalance created by the rapid spurt in the demand for HQM as against its almost static supply, the USA has to import HQM – the seed-corn technology from the LDCs. This transaction in HQM is made in such an evasive way that ultimately no price for the use of HQM is required to be paid to the country that supplies the HQM. A strange pattern of purchase indeed.

The imported seed-corn technology is then processed scientifically, pressed into service and exported through multi-nationals, mainly to the LDCs. Capital exports coupled with the export of technology on a huge scale to LDCs lead at least to three consequences: (1) Through the sale of costly and inappropriate western technology, the dependence of the LDCs on the DCs becomes enhanced. (2) The selling country becomes a *rentier* nation and gets richer by the fattening returns on investment, and royalties on the export of technology. Every year, the LDCs pay to the United States billions of dollars as dividends, fees and royalty, (3) The multinational corporations assume more significant role in translating into practice the neocolonial interests of the developed capitalist countries.

Instead of importing raw materials, the DCs are now importing brain from the LDCs without giving any compensation. This shows that, in international economic relations, the colonial-metropolitan nexus is still prevailing. The HQM is purchased as raw materials, turned into finished products and sold out to colonies at an exorbitant direct and indirect price. Thus, modern LDCs provide both the sources of raw materials (HQM) and the market for the goods purchased by the capitalist countries like America. This sort of technological imperialism leads to what can be called international "backwash effect", making the poor areas poorer and the rich areas richer.

It is very often claimed by the DCs that capitalist countries have been helping the LDCs by giving them aid and assistance. This apparently innocuous statement has to be taken with a caveat. Let us give it a close look. According to the UNCTAD report, US aid to the LDCs in 1970 amounted to $3.1 billion. As against this, the income gained by the USA through brain drain from the LDCs amounted to $3.7 billion.[13] This shows that whatever aid is given by the USA to the LDCs is more than compensated by the brain gain. The highest contribution to the net income gained by the USA is made by developing countries, particularly of Asia. The telling tale of exploitation is adequately revealed by the fact that, while the USA does not pay a single buck for the brain obtained from the LDCs, she is highly paid for the services of her experts who happen to be mostly the HQM from the countries. Thus, the leader cunningly rides on the laggards and wins the rat race of the capitalistic game.

If per capita education cost is taken to be $20,000 as is found in many careful studies, the developing countries' contribution to the USA becomes nearly $45 million every year without corresponding compensation. Thus, the LDCs' assistance to the USA becomes more overwhelming than American aid to these countries. It is in this sense that the concept of *reverse transfer of technology* from the LDCs to the DCs can be looked upon as a more detrimental dimension of the brain drain problem. As a matter of fact, the reverse flow of technology nullifies the tall claim for neo-imperialist aid to the Third World.

The DCs claim that they are trying to help the economic development of the LDCs, but, on the other hand, enacting immigration laws that encourage the flight of skilled labour. These are mutually contradictory activities in as much as brain drain jeopardises the technological base and hence the development tempo of such poor countries. It is a historical truism that no metropolitan country is ever really interested in the real development of the colonies. Had it been a policy to help the LDCs, the DCs would have allowed the immigration of ordinary unskilled labour. But they have altogether stopped the immigration of unskilled labour, and encourage the immigration of only skilled labour. The deliberate government policy facilitated the change-over from proletarian mass transfer to professional elite migration. The process of brain drain has become faster since the change in the Immigration laws in many developed countries.

In the field of technology, the western models are promiscuously applied. The software variety of technology transfer from the LDCs to the DCs is denied by the latter on the ground that knowledge is a universal public good. But it is strange that the same notion about knowledge is not entertained by the DCs in the matter of patent which is the embodiment of the universal knowledge. Out of 3 million current patents in the world, the LDCs hold only 30,000. If knowledge is a public good, why do the DCs charge for the export of technology which is based on knowledge? The answer to this question smacks of clear neo-imperialistic design which admits of no humanitarian or moral consideration about the struggle for economic development by the LDCs.

According to an estimate made by a Belgrade expert, over 300,000 experts from the LDCs migrated to the DCs in the past 10 years and most of them took up the jobs in the USA and Britain (see Adams, 1968). To educate these people, the LDCs invested $5 billion. This amount is higher than the amount of aid given by the USA and the UK ($4 billion) to the LDCs during the same period. This once again corroborates the notion of *Reverse Transfer of Technology*. Thus, between 1961 - 1972, UK, USA and Canada got brain aid of $4,400 billion from the LDCs. The study made by IDRC, Canada, reveals that the foreign aid of the these three countries to the LDCs amounted to only $46 billion. Even if we add the remittances, brain aid still far outweighs the foreign aid.

The DCs encourage brain drain from the LDCs mainly for the following reasons: (1) the workers are readily available 'on tap' without any education expenditure on them by DCs, (2) competent scholars can be had at a cheap rate, (3) during rough times, they can be retrenched, During the mid-1970s, economic recession in Europe forced about 1.2 million workers to return home, (4) employment does not involve any permanent commitment, (5) educational investment of a huge amount of money may be saved, (6) some amenities may be denied to foreign workers, and (7) without HQM, technology cannot be assimilated.

Be that as it may, brain drain from the LDCs has had many harmful consequences.[14] Brain drain raises the domestic wage in international professions, but the local professionals' wage remains the same. Hence, inequality is accentuated. Secondly, for want of HQM, it becomes difficult to properly utilise the modern technology. Thirdly, shortages of skilled manpower create dislocations and bottlenecks. Fourthly, brain drain brings about internal migration of HQM from villages to towns. This sort of internal brain drain disturbs unfavourably rural-urban professional distribution. Fifthly, the returnees bring in inappropriate technology, wrong model and inappropriate education from abroad. Over 40 per cent of R&D expenses in the DCs are on defence and space research to which brain drain is directed. The spillover effects do not benefit the LDCs. Lastly, the returnees and foreign experts increase the domestic wage, show preference for foreign items and, favour capital-intensive techniques and inappropriate ideologies and policies.

One negative phenomenon in the LDCs and for which the neocolonialism is largely responsible is the problem of brain drain.[15] The drain is caused by the greed of the DCs to accumulate more and more surplus. But the crucial cause is the neocolonial policy of buying HQM from the LDCs. In the face of scientific and technical revolution in the DCs, the demand for HQM is very rapidly increasing but not so much the supply. Hence, the wooing away of brain from the LDCs. Capitalist countries are making laws so that foreigners can become naturalised citizens of those countries very easily.

Brain drain is morally obtuse in at least two senses: (i) the strategic manpower of the LDCs is wooed away, and (ii) no compensation is paid to the brain-sending countries by the brain-receiving countries. The demoralising consequences erode the socio-psychological millieu and lead to national frustration. The leadership and the creative contribution to science, technology and development, which the emigrating people would have made, are lost by the sending country as a result of brain drain. The indirect costs of brain drain are many. Some of these are: slowdown in production, weakening of administrative and executive structures, rebuilding of skill, apathy of the state to skill formation and so on. By brain drain, the intellectual climate of the country is very much adversely affected. Without the intelligentsia, the idea of progress cannot be spread effectively. Thus, brain drain hampers social development, modernisation and economic growth.

True, remittances are repatriated in the cases of brain drain and brain overflow; but the remittances are not adequate, regular and compulsory, specially in the case of brain drain. It can be stated that remittances cannot lead to an adequate compensatory payment to the losers and these cannot cover the public and private cost of human capital involved in brain drain, albeit, these partly meet the private cost.

There should be a forum for redressing the unjust exploitative development policy of the capitalist world. The LDCs have to wage a historical struggle for emancipation in the real sense of the term and for the compensatory payment from the DCs against the outflow of the HQM. The brain-importing capitalist countries must be pressurised to pay for the brain, in the same way as physical capital import is paid. The migration HQM should be considered as an item in the balance of payment. The object of compensation would be to offset losses already incurred by a country; whereas the aim is to prevent those losses by regulating abnormal migration of HQM. But compensation has remained a mere idea which has never reached even the stage of preparation of bilateral or multilateral agreements. True, such an agreement has not been formally demanded by the LDCs. The LDCs do not demand compensation perhaps because of the fear that such a demand will reduce their aid from the USA. The Third World countries must jointly cooperate to pressurise the DCs to favourably consider the issue of compensation, and, if need be, the interposition of the UN and the socialist-minded countries may be sought in giving the idea of compensation a practical shape.

(v) World Monetary System and the New International Economic Disorder

Since the end of Second World War, the economic chasm between the developed countries (DCs) and LDCs has been gradually increasing and, of late, the economic distance between these two types of countries has gone beyond the level of tolerable proportions to the definite detriment of the LDCs. It is against the backdrop of this precarious world economic situation that the call for the New International Economic Order (NIEO) was given to save the sinking economy of the LDCs from the predatory exploitation and injustice by the DCs. The NIEO was an attempt to ensure justice, rights and equalities to the suffering LDCs to smoothen the process of world development through mutual help and cooperation between nations without any discrimination and discord. The NIEO has been sought in many areas of economic life like aid, trade, industrialisation and so on. One such important area where the NIEO was tried to be established is the area of international money and finance.

In the area of international monetary system, the LDCs have been facing various problems and difficulties and their monetary system is under constant threat and jeopardy. Some of these problems calling for a new monetary order for such countries can be briefly mentioned.

Firstly, the flow of funds to LDCs is constantly diminishing but the debt burden of these countries is constantly increasing. The problem is so familiar in recent times that it hardly needs any elaboration. These countries have become heavily indebted, and therefore, dependent on the developed capitalist countries who are obviously their creditors. This has a far-flung implication in that it has given rise to a pattern of dependent development on the part of the LDCs. Moreover, the export of capital by the DCs has also served the purpose of spreading capitalism in these poor nascent economies.

Secondly, the creation of international reserve has not helped the poor countries because adequate necessary real resources have not been transferred from DCs to LDCs.

Thirdly, it has been found that the allocation and distribution of special drawing rights (SDRs), the so-called international currency, have been very much skewed in favour of DCs and against LDCs. The distribution of SDRs has never been linked with the development plans of LDCs in spite of their repeated requests.

Fourthly, most of the LDCs have been experiencing heavy balance of payments deficit which has become chronic in nature. No serious attempt is made by the international monetary system to find a permanent solution to this malady which is affecting almost all the LDCs. On the other hand, there is an attempt to pass the buck and to follow a "beggar-thy-neighbour policy".

Fifthly, the LDCs have to pay a very high rate of interest and meet all harsh conditionalities for borrowing from the world monetary and financial institutions.

Sixthly, the LDCs have been facing a back-breaking rate of inflation and also sporadic partial recession. The domestic inflation is very often the manifestation of the exported inflation from the developed capitalist countries.

Seventhly, it has been very difficult for the LDCs to formulate a structure of operationally suitable exchange rate. Owing to external effects from abroad, the exchange rate of LDCs experiences sporadic fluctuations. It has also been very difficult for these countries to efficiently manage their reserves, for international price flex changes the value of these reserves often against the interest of these countries.

Lastly, the monetary and financial system set up at Bretton Woods has been very discriminatory and has served the interests of the developed capitalist countries. In particular, the role of IMF and World Bank has been step-motherly and discriminatory. These two institutions are unjust to LDCs and work as the agents of developed capitalist countries. Both these institutions try to intervene in the matter of formulation of domestic policies by LDCs. For instance, the IMF did a real havoc in damaging the internal monetary disciplines of the Philippines and Chile in the past. The IMF played a major role in the untimely devaluation debacle of the Philippines in 1992, and the World Bank virtually engineered the unwanted Indian devaluation of 1966. In the name of liberalisation, which is a part of conditionality, these financial twins open up the economies of LDCs to financial pimps and peddlers of the West. Let me elaborate some of the capitalist designs of these two financial giants in a bit more detail.

More often than not, the IMF follows a double standard. Like the World Bank, it is also a politically-oriented institution. In the name of stabilisation, it often suggests structural adjustment for LDCs, which often is not compatible with the development requirements of these countries. Its attempts to stabilise the poor countries has often led to destabilisation. The examples of Thailand, Philippines and Chile are before all of us. It has a

152

built-in oligarchic power structure. The decision-making process of the IMF and IBRD is heavily weighted in favour of the developed capitalist countries. These two major monetary institutions are controlled by the DCs, The United States alone has more than 20 per cent voting strength and the veto power. It is not surprising that the big members of the IMF often violated the Fund's rule regarding the alteration of par values of their currencies.

The IMF secured a dominant position for the USA by putting the dollar on par with gold making it the criterion and the basis of international monetary transactions.[16] The partisan attitude of the IMF is exposed from the fact that whereas in the case of massive borrowings by the UK in 1967 from the IMF, there was no condition imposed, but in the case of borrowing by LDCs like Brazil, India and Bangladesh, heavily damaging conditions were imposed. Before taking the IMF loan of $5.8 billion, India had to surreptitiously devalue her currency by about 14 per cent in September 1981. The devaluation, however, did not increase export but it increased the cost of imports.

There has been constant clamour from the LDCs for the restructuring of the IMF but it has been willy-nilly rejected by the DCs. As a matter of fact, the success of the IMF will depend upon the degree to which the LDCs can implement their development plans within the framework of financial stability.

The IMF is criticised on at least five grounds, e.g. inappropriateness, inadequacy, intrusiveness, neutrality and moral hazard. Its policy prescriptions, as the bailout package to some crisis-ridden Asian countries reveal, has remained inappropriate. The availability of resources and expertise with the IMF is inadequate. It has remained a discriminatory institution with regard to conditionalities for sanctioning loans and it has had the habit of interfering into the internal affairs of the economics and politics of the member countries. Its help also involves considerable **moral hazard** problem for the member countries not only because their dependencies on the IMF are enhanced but also because of the fact that through the wrong policies and misuse of power, it can aggravate the financial problems of LDCs. The bottom line is that the IMF has really failed to ameliorate the economic positions of developing countries on a sustainable basis. The experience of Tequila Crisis of 1994 – 95, the Asian flu of 1997 and the Russian Virus of 1998 has been a repeated pointer to the fact that the IMF has neither been able to forecast the financial crises nor able to prevent or tackle them properly.

The World Bank is another agent of the developed capitalist countries.[17] The Bank penetrates almost every sector of the borrowing country to take the stock of its internal weaknesses and strengths. It has been creating ground for the expansion of private capitalist sector by helping both the internal and external capitalist enterprises. The real motive of the Bank is not apolitical. The Bank, like the IMF, often influences internal policies and programmes of LDCs and dictates its own terms. It sustained an imperialist policy for Chile for whom it refused loans (see C. K. Wilber, *Soviet Model and Less Developed Countries*, p. 152 ff.). In 1965, the Bank refused India a loan for the reconstruction of state-owned iron and steel plant at Rourkela. Eugene Black wrote to the then Indian Finance Minister that in order to qualify for foreign aid, India should encourage private investment (see M. Kidron, *Foreign Investment In India*, 1965, p. 154). In fact, Clausen made it abundantly clear that the "...World Bank is not the Robinhood of the international financial set-up: it is a hard-headed unsentimental institution.....".

These political fringes apart, the Bank has been criticised as an institution which cannot supply adequate loans to LDCs, but charges too high a rate of interest and exercises too much, and at times, undesired control over the projects and the economy. The assessment of the Bank regarding the repaying capacity of the borrowing country has been criticised as too rigorous. Too much insistence on specific loans restricts the Bank's utility. Its main interest is to help the western capitalist aid-givers and spread capitalism in the soil of LDCs (C. P. Bhambri, *op. cit*).

For a number of reasons basically arising out of the non-comprising attitude of the DCs, the NIEO could not become successful, and it created many disorders by way of its implementation. Hence, it is dubbed by some as the New International Economic Disorder. In view of the rather disquieting situation prevailing in the world monetary system, a package of action programme on the establishment of the NIEO was taken up by the UN General Assembly. It will be in the fitness of things to state these measures in a summarised form here:

(a)   To check world inflation and its transfer to the LDCs
(b)   To eliminate the instability in international monetary system, particularly the uncertainty in exchange rate
(c)   To maintain the real value of currency reserves of the LDCs
(d)   To involve LDCs in all decision-making processes
(e)   To create additional liquidity, keeping in view its growing demand

(f)   To establish a link between the SDR allocation and the development finance requirements of LDCs

(g)   To promote the increasing net transfer of real resources from DCs to LDCs

(h)   To ensure that international financial institutions play the role of development financing banks without any fear and favour. Their lending policies should suit the needs of LDCs. Very poor countries should get special consideration and more favourable conditions in the matter of availability of loans

(i)   To renegotiate debt on a case-by-case basis with a view to concluding agreements on debt cancellation, moratorium and rescheduling the interest subsidisation.

The above listing of action programme incorporates most of the crucial aspects of the emerging monetary order; but it is by no means exhaustive. What is of paramount importance is the structural refurbishment of the whole international monetary system. The LDCs need to be given more representation in all the decision-making monetary processes. This will require the revision of the voting formula of the IMF and the World Bank. The LDCs should receive a free flow of liberalised official development assistance. To meet the needs of the LDCs, another Trust Fund can be created by selling the gold stock of the IMF. To ensure stable export income for the poor countries, *compensatory financing facility* needs to be liberalised. The extended financial flow to the deficit areas should be based on concessional terms and conditions, particularly for the areas of critical importance to LDCs. There is indeed a need for the new financial architecture. As the *theory of impossible trinity* asserts, a country cannot simultaneously maintain fixed exchange rate policy, independent monetary system and complete capital mobility. One has to sacrifice at least one of these mechanisms. As Frankel asserts, fixed exchange mechanisms, such a *dollarisation,* are suitable for small open economies or those desperate to import monetary stability, but the large economies should allow their currencies to float. The intermediate regimes between fixed and floating rates regimes are still appropriate for some economies, but the use of a particular mechanism has to be tailored to the unique circumstances of each country. It is also necessary for the Asian economies to put restriction on the inflow of short-term capital, the so-called hot money, till the financial markets become strong and resilient.

Another very crucial dimension of the new international financial architecture is the reform in the area of international finance. Various reforms proposals from both sovereign states and individual scholars have already been put forward and are still in the offing. The list is overwhelming but some of these that can be pinned down are: UK proposal of single super-regulator of financial markets, the French proposal of setting up of Interim Committee to oversee the operation of the IMF, George Soros's proposal of an International Debt Insurance Corporation, Jeffrey Garten's proposal of an International Central Bank, Henry Kaufman's proposal of an International Credit Rating Agency and Jeffrey Sachs's proposal of an International Bankruptcy Court. However, it is not the basic burden of the present section to analyse the relative merits, demerits and the applicability of these proposals here. Any attempt to elaborate on these will indeed take me too far afield.

The new order should, however, ensure stable but flexible exchange rate in order to create the framework necessary for the growth of trade of LDCs. All said and done, it needs to be emphasised that the new international monetary system has had to be established on the basis of equality, universality, stability and interdependence. It must recognise the conditions and the specific needs of the poor young nations for according a preferential treatment. The new international financial architecture must have transparency and accountability. It is time to realise that everything in the economic universe of discourse depends on everything else and all types of countries are equally represented in the international institutions.

(vi) Globalisation as Unequal Competition

Globalisation can be defined in various ways. It may mean universalisation of market economy and relations, globalised accumulation, global dependency and the growth of a world system. Globalisation constitutes the cross-national flows of investment, capital, goods and resources on wider scale and rather freely without any constraint. The concept of globalisation implicitly presumes the notion of win-win situation of mutuality of interdependence and gains.

Globalisation has many commonalities with imperialism in the earlier centuries. In this sense, globalism is not a new phenomenon. Some scholars look upon globalism as an extension and continuation of imperialism. For instance, British imperialism in the nineteenth century was based on the accumulation of capital, goods and resources from the colonies. One-third of British capital formation in the seventeenth century was based on the international slave trade.[18] The Mercantilist globalisation was the exploitation and accumulation of resources through trade and commerce.

The modern system of globalisation is different from the old system of globalisation in many important respects. In the past, the resource flows were mainly unidirectional, erratic and crude; in contradistinction to the earlier system, the recent system of globalisation is highly planned, systematic, subtle and more overwhelming, covering almost all aspects of economic life of the Third World countries. In such a system, as a matter of fact, there is an increasing amount dependence on the external flows of resources.

Whereas in the past, imperialism which was based on capitalist ideology made an attempt to spread it in the sphere of production in the dependent colonies, modern globalism is an attempt to globalise capitalism not only in the mode of production but also in other areas such as distribution. It is an attempt to will-nilly integrate the less developed countries into the framework of world capitalism to make them more dependent and to subject them to unequal competition. Because it is through this process that these countries can be exploited and substantial amount of surplus can be extracted from them.

In the new system of globalisation, there is the involvement of greater volume of physical and human capital, technology and a large scale organisational network. Capital inflow across the nation states amounts to several trillions of dollars daily. A large number of high quality manpower (HQM) from LDCs is also migrating and responding to changing job opportunities in the developed countries (DCs). Another important dimension of modern globalisation is the flow of information most quickly and in larger volume per unit of time. Modern globalisation is basically led by multinational corporations (MNCs). The production pattern of such corporations is extended to many countries simultaneously to take advantage of cheaper labour and organisation costs. Thus, in a sense, it creates more extended division of labour and markets.

Several salient features of modern globalisation become quite apparent. First, it is a programme of binding all individuals, institutions and nations into a common set of market relations. These relations, needless to say have their own laws of motion. Second, it is a calculated economic strategy of the capitalist economies and institutions to reinforce capitalist process of growth for these countries. Lastly, it is a means to extract surplus through the exploitation of cheap labour, HQM and resources of the Third World.

Given the knowledge of the classical economic system that capitalist system of growth ultimately leads to stationary state and that the rate of profit is ultimately to fall, some counteractive mechanism was needed by the modern capitalist countries to oppose these tendencies. The mechanism that is discovered is globalism which makes dependency more pronounced between the West and the Rest for capital, technology, investment and goods, and thus, creating an atmosphere more conducive for the sustaining growth of DCs. It should be noted here that the present-day DCs in general have a very low rate of economic growth, large scale fiscal imbalances, and growing unemployment and recession. Globalism is a device to solve these macro problems all at a time. Hence, for the speculators, financiers, investors and MNCs of DCs, globalisation is an *invevitable phenomenon.* It is the last stage of and the last attempt to survive capitalism.

There are indeed many channels and chains of globalisation. First, the message of globalism is spread through nation-states. These states are favoured by the DCs in many respects for supporting the ideology of globalism. Second, the so-called international organisations like the IMF and the IBRD through their structural adjustment and reform policies try to implement the programmes of globalisation, e.g. trade liberalisation, capital market liberalisation, privatisation, deregulation, free market policies and so on. Third, the comprador class which has received the western education and which is holding important positions in the administrative hierarchy of a country is an important channel for the spread of the idea of globalisation. Thus, the national development of India was led by a generation of western educated leaders such as Jawaharlal Nehru of India.[19]

Be that as it may, a number of factors has been found to be responsible for the growth of the recent wave of globalisation. First, high cost of production mainly due to increasing wages in DCs was a dent on their competitive advantage. The cost could be lowered by locating the production lines in LDCs where wage and organisational costs are lower. Second, cost reduction through global outsourcing of inputs will lead to profit maximisation. Third, over-accumulation of capital in DCs leads to declining marginal efficiency of capital. This tends to pauperise the western rentier class. Thus, globalisation of capital loaning is a sure way to earn higher interest income. Fourth, the opening up of capital markets in many developing countries gives enormous opportunities for the global financial players to enter into the lucrative speculative activities in these economies.

The liberalisation of the financial market is perhaps the most important determinant of globalisation. Equipped with better information system and better knowledge of the operation of financial markets, the players from the western countries can expect to have windfall gains through speculation as through the better management of financial investment and capital flows in the newly emerging markets. Globalisation is purported to take the advantage of newly emerging markets. Through all these, the MNCs can hope to maximise their market share and profit. Globalisation is a cash cow project for these corporations. These corporations are mainly the American corporations and the present century is euphemistically called the *American Century*. This is perhaps the reason why the United States was to become the main ideological and institutional centre of globalism.

But why is globalisation regarded so obnoxious? The reasons are not far to seek.

First, globalisation of capitalism is sure to intensify economic inequalities not only between the DCs and LDCs, but also between the capitalist and labouring classes in a state. Capitalism is based on the philosophy of production efficiency but neglects distributional equity. Under globalisation, capital will get more and labour will get less, much less than the value of its marginal productivity. So, there may be the perpetuation of relative poverty and inequality.

Second, unequal competition between DCs and LDCs in various fields of economic activities, e.g. banking in LDCs, would lead to more harm to LDCs in the form of unemployment, contraction, recession and so on. In the face of better technology and capital-intensive method of operation of DCs, the LDCs would not be able to compete effectively, and their income, output and employment will fall. On the other hand, the MNCs will gain substantially. Thus, there would not only be more dependency but also more poverty and backwardness in LDCs. The unequal competition generated and perpetuated by globalism is the most detrimental dimension of this phenomenon for LDCs.

Third, there would be more exploitation of labour, for the DCs will relocate their production centres to LDCs for minimisation of labour cost. And in the face of introduction of high-tech production, labour demand is likely to go down. Thus, there may be proletarianisation and immiserisation of labour. On the other extreme, due to monopoly-monosony relation in the market, surplus value from labour is likely to increase. The MNCs will have higher degrees of concentration and centralisation of capital, and these will virtually capture the market for capital and consumption goods in LDCs.

In fact, since the introduction of the idea of globalisation in the late eighties of the last century, the pauperisation of workers in the USA and England has intensified, and the living standards of Eastern Europe have fallen between 30 and 80 per cent.[20] The calorie intake in many LDCs has also substantially fallen between 1979 – 80 and 1995 – 97 (FAO Stat. 1999).

Fourth, the neo-liberal ideology like privatisation and deregulation unleashed by globalism has been creating many dislocations. Privatisation has converted public monopoly into private monopoly. It has led to excessive price escalations without corresponding quality improvements in many countries; but it has not led to new product development or development of new productive forces. It has brought about massive transfer of wealth from the public sector to the rich private capitalists. It has unnecessarily absolved the public sector of its responsibility towards social reproduction. It is no wonder, therefore, that the WHO has declared public health not as a *public good* but as a *private good*.

Finally, capitalist free market principle propagated through globalisation is not able to eradicate crisis. As a matter of fact, a capitalist economy is prone to have periodic recessions and crisis. Evidently, the inflow of capital in the absence of well-regulated and well-disciplined capital market may create havoc in LDCs. The Asian crisis in the nineties of the last century is a case in point. Needless, to say, under such a situation, the global players can bring home their capital safe or even with some speculative profit but the domestic economies of the affected countries are in peril.

All these will show that globalisation is likely to give rise to unequal competition between DCs and LDCs where the latter would be adversely affected. Thus, it would be better for the LDCs not to be carried by the western slogan of globalisation. It would be necessary to slowly open their economies for deregulation and liberalisation. Behind the philosophy of globalisation are the immense possibilities of exploitation of cheap and innocuous resources of LDCs: high quality manpower, skilled and semi-skilled labour, natural resources and the environment of LDCs which are priced much lower than the average world market price in such countries.

It is necessary at this stage of world development for the LDCs to be more selective in their choice of capital inflow, to impose some sort of tax on the speculative capital movement, to restrict the outflow of physical capital and high quality manpower, to raise the labour standard, to fix the decent minimum wages in collaboration with the ILO, and to improve the capabilities of human beings through appropriate entitlement and empowerment policies. Globalisation, after all, is a neo-colonialist strategy devised to extract surplus by the West from the Rest.

(vii) The West and the Rest: Between the End of History and the Clash of Civilisation

Speculations about international relations both at micro and macro-levels are indeed difficult to appreciate, more difficult to interpret and perhaps most difficult to make an appraisal of. However, even if many angels fear to tread in such uncertain roulette, political speculation remains always a hot subject of discussion. As the last century was drawing to a close, political *pundits* all over the globe had been busy in making all sorts of prognosis about the shape of things to come, and thus helping to formulate many hypotheses, theories and meta-theories. To name a few, these possibilities include decline of nation states, clash of civilisations and even the end of history.

In what follows, I will try to take a close critical look at the two most controversial prognostications of our times, namely, the *end of history* a la Fukuyama and the *clash of civilisations* a la Huntington, and in finale, I will make an attempt to provide an alternative paradigm that might seem to be plausible with the temper of time.

Drawing on the Hegelian concept, Francis Fukuyama stated that a situation like the end of history has ushered in the international sphere (*The National Interest*, Summer, 1989). The end of history marks the crowning success of economic and political liberal democracy which can be christened as the final form of human government.

Like Hegel, who believed that history ultimately culminates into an absolute moment where finally a rational form of society and state comes into being, Fukuyama also believes that the present state of international politics suggests that with the victory of free market capitalism and liberal democracy in our times, that final moment a la Hegel, marking the end of history has been reached. Karl Marx also suggested that the achievement of communism which can resolve all internal contradictions will indicate the end of history. But to Marx, this comes about only through a dialectical process of thesis, antithesis and synthesis.

161

The state that emerges at the end of history is essentially the most liberal one in the sense that it recognises and protects mankind's universal right to freedom and is based on people's will and consent. In such universal homogeneous states, all internal contradictions a la Marx get resolved and all human needs also get satisfied.

Fukuyama pontificates that the main challenges to liberalism and democracy, namely, fascism and communism, have already been annihilated from the international scenario. He asserts that class contradictions have been resolved successfully in the West, particularly in the USA, and *black poverty* is not the product of liberalism *per se.*

The end of history suggests the end of viable alternative ideology. In this connection, Fukuyama talks about two possible alternatives, namely, religion and nationalism, and observes that in the contemporary world, only Islam has offered a theocratic state as a political alternative to liberalism and communism. But he discards its viable potentiality by asserting that Islam cannot be significantly appealing to non-Muslims, and therefore, it is devoid of the quality of universality. Likewise, nationalism cannot also be a potent alternative because, *firstly*, it is not a single unified coherent phenomenon, and *secondly*, as can be seen from empiricism, nationalist movements are not buttressed by positive political programmes though they are backed by the negative desire of independence. Fukuyama believes that Marxism-Leninism has already become a nihilism as an ideology and it will imply the common marketisation of international relations and the diminution of the likelihood of major conflicts between states.

Fukuyama's thesis, however, is not free from criticism. But, spatial limitation here makes my criticism to be rather sketchy. Be that as it may, the concept of end of history may be interpreted in many ways and senses. For instance, in a sense, there was the end of history as claimed by Hegel in1806. But it revived again. Thus, history may end in one way and may be reborn in another way, with the growth of new ideology, new consciousness and new system. The end of history may be the beginning of another. In fact, the victory of liberal democratic capitalism does not imply the death of alternative ideologies. Many will agree to differ with Fukuyama's assertion that Marxism is now completely dead. Many political economists believe that Marxism might have failed as a model, but as methodology it will never fail. Among others, Ali A. Mazrui believes that as an ethic of distribution and the concern about economic inequalities, Marxism has not still been invalidated [*Journal of Malaysian Studies (Kajian Malaysia*), Vol. 11, No. 2, 1993, pp. 21-27].

Fukuyama is not right certainly in his assertion that in the liberal democratic capitalist system of the American type, all contradictions are already resolved and all human needs are satisfied. It is ludicrous that in the list of economic needs, he apparently includes only the easy access to stereos and VCRs. What about full employment, elimination of poverty and other class contradictions? Contrary to his belief, the capitalist world is still full of unresolved contradictions of various genres, particularly in the realm of economics. In the true sense of the term, freedom, which implies man's conscious control over the socio-economic conditions of life has never been present under capitalism, nor will it be in the future. The final politico-economic form may not indeed be the last form indicating the end of history. Fukuyama merely speaks about the political order and not human values. Contrary to the achievement of human desideratum a la Fukuyama, capitalism has hopelessly failed to improve upon human capabilities through empowerment and entitlement. The neglect of human development is the most serious failure of capitalism.

Furthermore, given the constraints of our bounded rationality, the confidence limits of our ignorance, limited information, education and human vulnerability, democracy may not be the best form of government. Even Aristotle put it in the category of perverted form of government. Kenneth Arrow, a Nobel Laureate, has demonstrated in his *Impossibility Theorem* that it is impossible to have rational choice under democracy.

On the question of the possibility of alternative ideology, the importance of Islam has indeed very elaborately been analysed by Ali A. Mazrui. Let me reserve this aspect for discussion in the later part of this section.

Samuel P. Huntington's main thesis is that the clash of civilisations will now dominate global politics (see, *Foreign Affairs*, Summer, 1993, pp. 22-49). He hypotheses that the fundamental source of conflict in this new world will not be primarily ideological or economic. In the past, as Huntington observes, the conflicts between kings, nation-states and ideologies were primarily conflicts within western civilisation. With the end of the Cold War, international politics moves out of the western sector, and its main focus becomes the interaction between the western and non-western civilisations, and people and governments now become the shapers of history rather than mere objects of history.

The groupings of countries in terms of different worlds are no longer relevant, but a more meaningful grouping would be on the basis of civilisations. A civilisation is the highest cultural grouping of people. In other words, a civilisation may comprise many sub-cultural entities, and indeed many nation states. Huntington asserts that conflict of the future will occur along the cultural fault lines. Cultural animosities are deeply rooted in history, and aggravated by the forces of economic modernisation which is separating people from local identities. Religious fundamentalism then fills up the gap and transcends national boundaries to protect the interest of the civilisation from the onslaught of another civilisation and the result may be a clash. In fact, there are many causes of clash of civilisations, namely, religious differences, political factors, economic differences, dependency, unequal interactions, exploitation *et al.*

With the end of the Cold war, cultural commonalities have been successfully able to overcome ideological differences among the nation states of the same civilisation. The clash is possible both at micro and at macro levels. Huntington mentions that conflict along the fault line between Western and Islamic civilisations at the micro level has been going on for 1300 years, and the military interaction between the West and Islam is unlikely to end, rather it could become more virulent. Conflicts of civilisations are also to be found between Hindus and Muslims, China and America and between Japan and the United States. Cultural differences, according to Huntington, exacerbate economic conflicts.

The kin-country syndrome is gradually emerging in international conflicts. Thus, during the Gulf War, Saddam Hussein invoked Islamic appeal by depicting it as the war between west and Islam. As a matter of fact, differences in economic, military, political and institutional powers between the west and non-west is a potent source of conflict. The non-western states may combine to challenge the western power, and there may be a clash of civilisation. In this connection, Confucian-Islamic connection is a case in point. There may be the possibility of conflicts between the West and the Rest (see, Kishore Mahbubani, *The National Interest*, Summer, 1992) that may lead to wars. In the immediate future, conflicts are likely between the west and the several Islamic-Confucian states. Huntington advocates, therefore, curbing of economic and military powers of non-western states and strengthening of these powers for the western states.

Contrary to the belief of Huntington that grouping of the world in terms of political or economic achievement is irrelevant, it appears that the whole concept of the modern world is firmly standing on the two legs of the developed capitalist countries (DCs) and the less developed countries (LDCs). In fact, culture, civilisations and ideologies are merely superstructures based on the consciousness of economic determinism. The identity of civilisations will remain less important a force than economic and political base of the state. Huntington is wrong when he asserts that interactions among people will enhance civilisation consciousness that will lead to animosity. It may, on the other hand, lead to better understanding and relations. Equally wrong is his notion that the processes of economic modernisation and social change are separating people from local identities. This is not inevitable and far less a plausible cause of conflict. According to Huntington, cultural differences will exacerbate economic conflict. The cart is indeed put before the horse! In fact, what is more probable is that economic self-interest may ultimately lead to cultural conflict.

What will be the role of politics, religion and gender? Will there be conflicts between secular civilisation and religious civilisations? What will be the constructive actions available for the Muslim World? Ali A. Mazrui considers Islam to be the inheritor and torch-bearer of the Abrahamic tradition in history. Through Pan-Islamic movement, Islam can be transformed into a world power, Islam has always had a keen sense of historical consciousness, and it is the maker of history. He strongly believes that the role of Muslims as shapers of history will continue through the processes of democratisation of Islam and Islamisation of democracy (*Kajian Malaysia*, Vol. 11, No.2, 1993). The Muslim world may be the active participants of a reverse evolution to a world of less statehood, greater social intimacy and declining secularism. Professor Mazrui very passionately upholds the view that in the 21st Century, the balance of power will shift towards Asia where religion and politics will be reunited in new ecumenical ways.

The present scenario of world political economy suggests that at the macro-level, the line of conflict would be sharper between DCs and LDCs and the conflict would be fundamentally sharpened by the economic disparities between these two groups of countries, arising mainly out of the new international economic disorders. The DCs will impose many restrictions to curb the rising militarism and economic power of LDCs. This will induce the LDCs to be far more united, retaliatory and reactionary by forgetting their cultural differences which may find expression at the macro-levels. In the short-term, the clash of economic determinism is likely to be very decisive. However, with deindustrialisation and decaying economic power in the long-run, the DCs will be like Samsons with their locks shorn in the battle of politico-economic supremacy, and the LDCs with the growing economies will emerge more dominant in the global scenario. A detailed analysis of this outline here will take me too far afield and would require perhaps another fresh attempt to threadbare.

Notes

1.	Singer, Hans W. (1997), "The 1960s: A Decade of Optimism", *Development*, Vol. 40, No. 1, March, pp. 16-17.
2.	Wignaraja, Ponna (1997), "The 1980s: Seeds for Change", *Development*, March, pp. 81-83.
3.	Esteva, Gustavo and Madhu, Suri Prakash, (1998), "Beyond Development, What?", *Development in Practice*, August, p. 46.
4.	The UNCTAD Report (1974) observed that US foreign aid to LDCs amounted to $3.1 billion in 1970; but the income by the United States through brain drain, the seed-corn technology, amounted to $3.7 billion in the same year. The study makes it quite clear that it is really the poor countries which are, on balance, aiding the rich developed countries, and not the other way round (vide, Ghosh, B.N., "Brain Drain" in Phillip O'Hara (ed.), *Encyclopedia of Political Economy*, London & New York, Routledge, 1999).
5.	Harcourt, Wendy (1997), "The Search for Social Justice", *Development*, Vol. 40, No. 1, pp. 5-8.
6.	O'Connell, Helen (1997), "The 1990s: New Alliances, New Directions", *Development*, March, pp. 119-20.
7.	Hicks, Norman and Paul Streeten (1979), "Indicators of Development", *World Development*, June.
8.	Morris, D. (1979), *Measuring the Condition of the World's Poor: The Physical Quality of Life Index*, Pergamon, New York.
9.	Sen, Amartya (1992), *Inequality Reexamined*, Harvard University Press, Cambridge.
10.	_____ (1986), "Poverty and Entitlement", in *Poverty and Famine: An Essay on Entitlement and Deprivation*, Clarendon Press, Oxford.
11.	*Brain drain* has not been properly defined in the literature. It is very often confused with *brain overflow*. While the former is from the employed category, the latter is from the unemployed human capital stock. The literature on brain drain is fairly extensive. Since it is not possible here to quote the entire body of literature, we mention Walter Adams (ed.), *The Brain Drain*, Macmillan, New York, 1968, which contains a fairly large number of contributions. See also B. N. Ghosh and Rama Ghosh, *Economics of Brain Migration*, Deep & Deep Publications, Delhi, 1982.
12.	The loss can be interpreted in terms of the loss of educational investment, the cost of relinquished alternatives, the loss of life-time income, the loss of interest on invested capital and also the social loss. The external diseconomies involved in brain drain are really very high.
13.	Govt. of India (1975, 1976), *Economic Survey*, New Delhi, and *Mainstream* No. 16, 1974.
14.	Jolly, R. and Dudley, Seers (1972), "Brain Drain and the Development Process" in G. Ranis (ed.), *The Gap Between Rich and Poor Nations*, Macmillan, London.

15. Tarabrin, E. A. (ed.) (1982), *Neocolonialism and Africa*, Progress Publisher, Moscow.
16. Ghosh, B. N. (1985), *Political Economy of Neocolonialism in Third World Countries*, Sterling Publishers, N. Delhi, p. 40 ff.
17. Bhambri, C. P. (1982), *World Bank and India*, Vikas Publication, N. Delhi.
18. James Petras (1999), "Globalisation: A Critical Analysis", *Journal of Contemporary Asia*, Vol. 29, No. I, p. 5.
19. Ozey Mehmet (2000), "Globalisation as Westernisation: A Post-colonial Theory of Global Exploitation" in B.N. Ghosh (ed.), *Contemporary Issues in Development Economics*, Routledge, London.
20. James Petras (1999), op. cit. p. 28.

Bibliography

Aghevli, B. B. and Khan, M. S. (1970), "Inflationary Finance and the Dynamics of Inflation: Indonesia (1951-72)", *American Economic Review*, 67 (3).

Amin, S. (1974), *Accumulation on a World Scale*, Harvester Press, Sussex.

Amin, S. (1976), *Unequal Development*, Harvester Press, Sussex.

Amin, S. (1977), *Imperialism and Unequal Development*, Harvester Press, Sussex.

Amin, S. (1983), "Expansion or Crisis of Capitalism?", *Third World Quarterly*, April.

Baran, Paul A. (1957), *The Political Economy of Growth*, Penguin Books, England.

Baran, Paul A. and Paul M. Sweezy (1966), *Monopoly Capitalism*, Monthly Review Press, USA.

Bardhan, Pranab (1982), "Agrarian Class Formation in India", *Journal of Peasant Studies*, Vol. X, No. 1.

Barnet, S. and Muller, R.(1974), *Global Rich: The Power of Multinational Corporations*, Simon and Schuster, New York.

Barrat Brown, M. (1974), *The Economics of Imperialism*, Middlesex, Penguin.

Basu, K. (1985), *The Less Developed Economy*, Oxford University Press.

Bauer, P. T. (1971), *Dissent on Development*, London.

Bernstein, H. (1979), "Sociology of Underdevelopment Versus Sociology of Development", in D. Lehmann (ed.), *Development Theory: Four Critical Studies*, Frank Cass.

Bhaduri, A. (1983), *The Economic Structure of Backward Agriculture*, Academic Press, London.

Bhagwati, J. N. (1958), "Immiserizing Growth", *Review of Economic Studies*.

Bhambri, C. P. (1982), *World Bank and India*, Vikas Publications, Delhi.

Black, E. R. (1960), *The Diplomacy of Economic Development*, Harvard University Press, Mass.

Bottomore, T. (1983), *A Dictionary of Marxist Thought*, Oxford University Press, London.

Brenner, R. (1977), "The Origins of Capitalist Development: A Critique of Neo-Smithian Marxism", *New Left Review*, No. 104, July-August.

Brown, M. B. (1976), *The Economics of Imperialism*, Penguin Books, London.

Cardoso, F. H. (1972), "Dependency and Development in Latin America", *New Left Review*, July-August.

Cardoso, F. H. and Faletto, E. (1979), *Dependency and Development in Latin America*, University of California Press, USA.

168

Chicherov, A. I. (1971), *India: Economic Development from Sixteenth to Eighteenth Centuries*, Nanka Publishing House, Moscow.

Choudhury, Sudip, (1979), "Financing of Growth of Transnational Corporations in India", *Economic and Political Weekly*, August 18.

Cohen, B. J. (1973), *The Question of Imperialism: The Political Economy of Dominance and Dependence*, Basic Books, New York.

Corbridge, Stuart (1986), *Capitalist World Development*, MacMillan, London.

Dore, E. and Weeks, J. (1977), "International Exchange and Causes of Backwardness", *Latin American Perspective*.

Dutton, D. (1971), "A Model of Self-Generating Inflation: The Argentine Case", *Journal of Money, Credsit and Banking*, 3 (2).

Emmanuel, A. (1972), *Unequal Exchange*, Monthly Review Press, New York.

Fagen, R. H. (1983), "Theories of Development", *Monthly Review*, Sept., 1983.

Frank, A. G. (1966), "The Development of Underdevelopment", *Monthly Review*, Sept.

Frank, A. G. (1967), *Capitalism and Underdevelopment in Latin America*, Monthly Review Press, USA.

Frank, A. G. (1969), *Latin America: Underdevelopment or Revolution*, Monthly Review Press, USA.

Frank, A. G. (1972), *Lumpenbourgeoisie and Lumpendevelopment*, Monthly Review Press, USA.

Frank, A. G. (1977). *On Capitalist Underdevelopment*, Oxford University Press.

Frank, A. G. (1979), *Dependent Accumulation and Underdevelopment*, Monthly Review Press, New York.

Friedsman, E. and Mark Selden (eds.) (1970), *America's Asia*, Pantheon.

Friedsman, W. G. and Kamanoff, G. (eds.), (1961), *Joint International Business Ventures*, Columbia University Press, New York.

Furtado, C. (1964), *Development and Underdevelopment*, University of California Press, California.

Galenson, W. and Leibenstein, H. (1955), "Investment Criteria , Productivity and Economic Growth", *Quarterly Journal of Economics*, August.

Gandhi, M. (1991), "Politics of Foreign Aid", *Illustrated Weekly of India*, 30-31, March.

Ghatak, Subrata (1981), *Monetary Economics in Developing Countries*, Macmillan, London.

Ghosh, B. N. (1985), *Political Economy of Neocolonialism in Third World Countries*, Sterling Publishers, New Delhi.

Ghosh, B. N. (1990), *Political Economy: A Marxist Approach*, Macmillan.

Ghosh, B. N. and Ghosh, R. (1982), *Economics of Brain Migration*, Deep and Deep Publications, New Delhi.

Ghosh, S. K. (1984), "Marx on India", *Monthly Review*, Jan.

Gibson, B. (1980), "Unequal Exchange: Theoretical Issues and Empirical Findings", *Review of Radical Political Economics*, Fall.

169

Goulet, A. (1976), "The Suppliers and Purchasers of Technology", *International Development Review*, Nov. 3, 1976.

Govt. of India (1965), *Report of Monopoly Inquiry Commission*, Delhi.

Govt. of India (1975), *Report of the Committee on Drugs and Pharmaceutical Industry*, New Delhi.

Griffin, K. B. and Enos, J. L. (1970), "Foreign Assistance: Objectives and Consequences", *Economic Development and Cultural Change*, Vol. 18, No. 3.

Griffin, K. and Gurley, J. (1985), "Radical Analyses of Imperialism, the Third World, and the Transition to Socialism: A Survey Article", *Journal of Economic Literature*, Sept.

Gulalp, H. (1983), "Frank and Wallerstein Revisited", in P. Limqueco and Bruce McFarlane (eds.), *Neo-Marxist Theories of Development*, Croom Helm, Kent.

Gulalp, H. (1986), "Debate on Capitalism and Development", *Capital and Class*, Spring.

Gupta, Neena (1975), "Foreign Monopolies Dominate Indian Drug Industries", *Social Scientist*, July.

Habib, Irfan, (1969) "Problems of Marxist Historical Analysis", *Enquiry*, Monsoon.

Hamaza, A. (1964), "Imperialism: Old and New", *The Socialist Register*.

Harris, D. J. (1972), "On Marx's Schema of Reproduction and Accumulation", *Journal of Political Economy*, Vol. 85.

Hensman, R. (1976), "Capitalist Development and Underdevelopment: Towards a Marxist Critique of Samir Amin", *Economic and Political Weekly*, April, 17.

Hobsbawm, E. (1964), *Pre-Capitalist Economic Formation*, Lawrence & Wishart.

Howard, M. C. and King, J. E. (1975), *The Political Economy of Marx*, Longmans, London, 1975.

Hyson, Charles, D. and Strout, A. M. (1968), "Impact of Foreign Aid on US Import", *Monthly Review*, Jan-Feb.

Hyter, Teresa (1971), *Aid as Imperialism*, Penguin Books, Harmondsworth, Middlesex.

Jameson, K. P. and Wilber, C. K. (eds.) (1979), *Directions in Economia Development*, University of Notre Dame Press, Indiana.

Janvery, A. D. and Karmer, F. (1979), "Limits of Unequal Exchange", *Review of Radical Political Economics*, Winter.

Kay, Geoffrey (1975), *Development and Underdevelopment: A Marxist Analysis*, Macmillan, London.

Kidron, M. (1965), *Foreign Investment in India*, Oxford University Press, London.

Klein, L. R. and Su, V. (1978), "Simulated Protectionism According to Project Link", Paper presenteds to the Meeting of Project Link, U. N. (Hq.).

Klochkovsky, L. L. (1978), *Economic Neocolonialism*, Progress Publishers, Moscow.

Laclau, E. (1971), "Feudalism and Capitalism in Latin America", *New Left Review*, May-June.

Lall, S. (1973), "Is Dependence a Useful Concept in Analysing Underdevelopment?", *World Development*, Vol. 2, No. 11.

Lean, Geoffrey (1978), *Rich World, Poor World*, Allen and Unwin, London.

Lehmann, D. (eds.), (1979), *Development Theory: Four Critical Studies*, Frank Cass.

Lenin, V. (1964), *Imperialism: The Highest Stage of Capitalism*, Collected Works, Moscow.

Leontief, W. *Domestic Production and Foreign Trade*, Proceedings of American Philosophical Society, IF No. 4.

Levin, I. V. (1964), *The Export Economies*, Harvard University Press.

Limqueco, P. and Bruce McFarlane (eds), (1983), *Neo-Marxist Theories of Development*, Croom Helm, Kent.

McNamara, Robert S. (1973), *One Hundred Countries, Two Billion People: The Dimensions of Development*, Praeger Publishers, New York.

Magdoff, H. (1968), "The Age of Imperialism", *Monthly Review*, Vol. XX.

Marx, K. (1853), "British Rule in India", *New York Daily Times*, 25 June.

Marx, K. (1853), "Future Results of British Rule in India", *New York Daily Tribune*, 22 July.

Marx, K. (1970), *A Contribution to the Critique of Political Economy*, Progress Publishers, Moscow.

Marx, K. (1973), *Grundrisse*, Penguin Books, Harmondsworth & Ramdon House, New York.

Marx, K. (1975), *Collected Works*, Lawrence & Wishart, London.

Marx, K. (1977), *Capital*, Vols. I, II, III, Lawrence & Wishart, London.

Marx, K. and Friedsrich Engels (1975), *Selected Correspondence*, Progress Publishers, Moscow.

Meier, G. M. (1984), *Leading Issues in Economic Development*, Oxford University Press, London.

Mohri, Kenzo (1979), "Marx and Underdevelopment", *Monthly Review*, April.

Molnar, T. (1965), *Africa: A Political Travelogue*, New York.

Morgan, Theodore, (1975), *Economic Development*, Harper and Row, New York.

Myrdal, G. (1964), *Economic Theory and Underdeveloped Regions*, Methuen & Co Ltd., London.

Myrdal, G. (1968), *Asian Drama*, Vol. I, Allen Lane, Penguin Press, New York.

Nash, M. (eds.) (1976), *Essays on Economic Development and Cultural Change, in Honour of Bert F. Hoselitz*, University of Chicago Press, USA.

Nehru, Jawaharlal (1947), *Glimpses of World History*, Macmillan, New York.

Nkrumah, K. (1969), *Neocolonialism: The Last Stage of Imperialism*, Thomas Nelson and Sons, London.

171

Nove, A. (1974), "On Reading Andre Gunder Frank", *The Journal of Development Studies*, Vol. 10, Nos. 3 and 4 April-July.

Nukhovich, E. (1980), *International Monopolies and Developing Countries*, Progress Publishers, Moscow.

Oxaal, R. L. et al (eds.) (1975), *Beyond the Sociology of Development: Economy and Society in Latin America and Africa*, Routledge and Kegan Paul, London, 1975.

Palma, G. (1978), "Dependency: A Formal Theory of Underdevelopment or A Methodology for the Analysis of Concrete Situations of Underdevelopment?", *World Development*, Vol. 6.

Patnaik, Utsa (1972), "On the Mode of Production in Indian Agriculture: A Reply", *Economic and Political Weekly*, Sept., 30.

Pavlov, V. I. (1978), *Historical Premises of India's Transition to Capitalism*, Nanka Publishing House, Moscow.

Payer, Cheryl (1974), *The Debt Trap*, Monthly Review Press, USA.

Pearson, Lester B. (1970), *Patterns In Development*, London, 1970.

Poete, Antonia De , "As Western Ships Sail on in Convoy", *The New York Times*, May 9, (1979).

Prebisch, R. (1950), *Economic Development in Latin America and its Principal Problems*, UN Department of Economic Affairs, Lake Success, New York 1950.

Prebisch, R. (1959), "Commercial Policies in Underdeveloped Countries", *American Economic Review*.

Radetzki, Marian (1973), *Aid and Development: A Handbook for Small Donors*, London.

Roemer, John (ed.) (1986), *Analytical Marxism*, Cambridge University Press, Cambridge.

Roxborough, I. (1979), *Theories of Underdevelopment*, Macmillian, London.

Saini, M. K. (1981), *Politics of Multinationals*, Geetanjali Prakashan, New Delhi.

Samuelson, Paul (1957), "Wages and Interest: A Modern Discussion of Marxian Economic Models", *American Economic Review*, Vol. 47.

Santos, D. T. (1969), "The Crisis of Development Theory and the Problem of Dependence in Latin America", *Siglo, XXI*.

Santos, D. T. (1970), "The Structure of Dependence", *American Economic Review*, May.

Schultz, T. W. (1981), *Investing in People*, University of California Press, USA.

Schumacher, A. (1973), *Small is Beautiful*, Blond and Briggs.

Servan Schreiber, (1968), *The American Challenge*, Harmondsworth, Penguin.

Shildkrut, V. A. (1963), *Price Problems of the World Capitalist Market*, Moscow.

Singer, H. (1950), "The Distribution of Gains Between Investing and Borrowing Countries", *American Economic Review*, May.

Singer, H. and Javeds Ansari (1978), *Rich and Poor Countries*, George Allen and Unwin, London.

172

Smith, A. (1937), *The Wealth of Nations*, The Modern Library Edition.

Smith, S. (1980), "The Ideas of Samir Amin: Theory of Tautology?", *Journal of Development Studies*, Oct.

Sternberg, M. (1974), "Dependency, Imperialism and the Relations of Production", *Latin American Perspectives*, Vol. I, No. I.

Sunkel Osvaldo. (1973), "Transnational Capitalism and National Integration", *Social and Economic Studies*, Special Number, March.

Sunkel Osvaldo. (1989), "National Development Policy and External Dependency in Latin America", *Journal of Development Studies*, Oct.

Swamy, S. (1971), *Indian Economic Planning*, Vikas Publications, Delhi.

Szalaifer, H. (1983), "Economic Surplus and Surplus Value: An Attempt at Comparison", *Review of Radical Political Economics*, Spring.

Tarabrin, E. A. (1978), *Neocolonialism and Africa*, Progress Publishers, Moscow.

Trotsky, L. (1934), *The History of the Russian Revolution* (Translated by Max Eastman), Victor Gellancz.

U. N. (1978), *World Economic Survey*, New York.

UNCTAD (1967), *A Review of International Trade and Development*, TD/5.

UNCTAD (1972), *Restrictive Business Practices*, T/p122/Supplement-I, Santiago De Chile, Jan. 1.

Uphoff N. T. and Ilchman W. F. (eds.) (1972), *The Political Economy of Development*, University of California Press, USA.

Vakhrushev, Vasily (1973), *Neocolonialism: Methods and Manoeuvres*, Progress Publishers, Moscow.

Wallerstein, I. (1974), *The Modern World System*, Academic Press, New York.

Warren, B. (1973), "Imperialism and Capitalist Industrialisation: Myths of Underdevelopment", *New Left Review*, Sept.-Oct.

Warren, B. (1982), *Imperialism: The Pioneer of Capitalism*, Verso.

Wilber, C. K. (ed.) (1973), *Political Economy of Development and Underdevelopment*, Random House, USA.

Wyrick, B. (1962), "Export Contamination: US Style", *Indian Express*, Feb. 28.

Index